What People Are Saying About Morgana Rae's Financial Alchemy®

"When I did the work, and completed all the exercises in her book, and was open to learning about money in a new way, **my bank account started growing!** I was surprised that **my emotions about money were the elixir**. How did I feel about money? What I learned from Morgana's workbook was that it was **more magical for me to feel how money felt about me.** I would definitely recommend this workbook for anyone who wants to create more financial success in their life. It definitely worked for me!"– *Pirie Jones Grossman, E-Entertainment Host, TEDx Speaker, Best-Selling Author and award-winning Master Coach, Sun Valley, Idaho*

"I purchased your book, and it literally turned my life around! As an entrepreneur, I knew I could do better, but I had sticky beliefs. Well, after meeting my Money Honey things turned around quickly! I had a **$21,000 month in June**, and so far **July has brought $12,500 my way**. I adore my Money Honey! Thank you, Morgana!!! **You transformed my life!!**" – *Kim Robinson, California*

"**Over $20,000 has come to me in different, unexpected** ways outside my regular income, since I have been using the *Financial Alchemy*® method. The experience has given me the **confidence to move ahead** on a major life dream of mine."– *Katie Curtin, Toronto*

"I created a new relationship with money and just a **few days later I received almost $4,000**. Some of this money I had given up on collecting. It came from multiple sources all on the same day. Great stuff!!! I am excited and love this new relationship. Your financial alchemy program is so very powerful yet simple and fun. Again, Thank You Morgana." – *Jason Hignite, Liberty League International*

"**This is soooo different**. When I just follow Morgana's instructions week to week, EVEN WHEN THEY DON'T SEEM TO MAKE SENSE, **I manifest so easily**, including those things that are completely out of my control. Now, I just keep marveling at what's happening for me and my loved ones. The best part is that I'm having so much fun! Yeah, I said it, this workbook is fun!" – *Darby Trotten*

"This work, you, have been so **life changing** for me. I teach law of attraction and yet money always eluded me. Until now...now it's rolling in!" – *Connie Nash*

"I got more from *Financial Alchemy* than every other book, class and training I've taken put together." – *Cheryl Woodhouse*

"Your Financial Alchemy book is truly fabulous. **This is seriously, the one book that has helped me keep on track...not just for money, but for all of my life goals.** I'm only now starting my second quarter and I have to say it's created the space for major healing and change to occur." – *Brigitta Dau, Los Angeles*

"I'm a newly self-employed artist and was journaling about how the Financial Alchemy chapter made me look at money in a whole new–and admittedly much healthier–way. The phone rang during my writing and voila! It was **a big job.** I even received an inquiry from a potential client that I've been trying to land for quite a while! **It surely is 'alchemy'!**" – *Alesia Zorn, Portland, Oregon*

"Major thanks for your program. **It allowed me to take the past year off without financial worries.** Giving me plenty of time to decide what I wanted to do with my life." – *Ann Rusnak, Ohio*

"I asked my 'Money Honey' again for gifts from the Universe and **got a repeat $2,000 booking.**" – *Anna K, New York City*

"Reading this book is the **most fun and lucrative experience** I've ever had. **Recommend this book to all my friends!**" – *Cat Williford, author of the Ovarian Chronicles*

"Morgana Rae is Magical! Her Financial Alchemy program and workbook helped us to let go of negative beliefs around financial and material wealth, replacing them with **perfect control over our finances**." – *Aime McCrory, California*

"How quickly my life has changed. I had a client **call and give me $300** on Monday and another client ordered more promotional materials on Tuesday, and yesterday my check from Borders stores came in. Wow – I'm loving this new relationship with Money – thank you!" – *Acaysha Dolphin, President for Society of Authors and Writers*

"Your *Financial Alchemy* Workbook is great. I don't go a day without using it. It takes just a few minutes, and the results are wonderful. I am in sales, and I have **consistently surpassed my monthly targets with ease**. Your products have allowed me to create a healthy relationship with money. I find money exciting and rewarding to deal with now. I look forward to successes every day. The best part is that your methodology **has improved other areas of my life as well**." – *Joseph Kraut, Ann Arbor, Michigan*

"A delinquent client paid me, I signed on two new clients, had conversations with people about money that I would never have comfortably had before, and experienced **the joy of NOT feeling the icy-cold, pit-of-my-stomach fear sensation I've had for years**. I insisted that someone follow through on a commitment she made to me...one that was very uncomfortable for me to pursue...and she came through!" – *B.J. King, Washington D.C.*

"Life changing. It says it's about money - and it is, but it's also about love and relationships. I've given copies of it to friends." – *Shari Carey, Texas*

"Only been using the workbook for 2 weeks and already my income has increased drastically and I'm feeling much more in control of my finances." – *Daryl A. Denman, Texas*

"Through *Financial Alchemy*, I was able to create a whole new relationship with money. This relationship not only allows me to show up as a wealthy, empowered, successful woman, but gently demands it. And this has in turn rippled out into every area of my life so that **I am now a wealthy woman in every sense of the word**. Thank you, Morgana and Financial Alchemy. I am so grateful." – *Sarah Hoskin Clymer, Colorado*

"I just had to share this with you. I cleared my money monster and invited my money honey in last week and this morning I hit a wobbly (a bit of old money monster stuff) and my money honey said that he loves me, and I deserve happiness and how he can't stand to see me sad. He showed me a suitcase full of money and said it was for me. **Literally THREE HOURS LATER**, I received a loan **to PAY MY DEBTS IN FULL!!!** Thank you Morgana, I look forward to my new relationship with money and all the adventures that we will have." – *Tanja Jaeger, South Africa*

"I'm seeing **success beyond my wildest dreams**… I'm constantly **blown away at the business and new clients that I'm attracting**… The thought goes through my head many times a day now 'I do live a **charmed life.**'" – *Lavon Lacey, owner of Quantum Entertainment, Inc., Atlanta, Georgia*

"**Surpassed my expectations. Effective and inspiring. Change for the better occurs. This is a second year and second time purchased book. It is worth it.**" – *Sheila Chandler*

"Each time I do the workbook, I realize even more about myself than ever. For one, **I no longer have to beat myself up.** I can forgive and move on. Secondly, **I have all the time I need to accomplish and improve my life.** It is no longer a rush. All I have to do is stick to it and keep moving. Third, despite fears, doubts, anxieties or apprehensions, I just let them pass and do what I want anyhow. It is not that these things won't present themselves, but my reaction to them has changed. Lastly, **I am more powerful than I realized** in the past. Power is not something you take from someone, because you have it yourself…each of us!" – *Dorothy Davis, Ann Arbor, Michigan*

"**The most amazing thing happened!** Shortly after changing my way of thinking and discussing things more openly with my 'money honey'… I was blessed with a **pleasant surprise**: I was informed that due to a lawsuit regarding overtime payment with a rival company to my previous employer, I will be receiving **retroactive overtime payment from the last 3 years!** Based on my calculations, **the amount should be 6 figures!!!** Omigosh!!! I've already gotten in touch with my former HR and will be in the process of filling out the forms shortly! This is such a wonderful blessing!" – *Gerry G., Toronto, Ontario*

"I love that the book starts with **the most powerful process I have done around money!** I have shifted my relationship to money. **Money loves me and it comes to me with so much more ease** and gratitude now. Thank you, Morgana Rae!" – *Gary Olsen, Tucson, Arizona*

"The simplest coaching program, easy to read and follow and yet brilliant. I am loving every bit of it; it makes so much sense." – *Betty Dees*

"Last week both my husband and I commented that **everything was so effortless that it was almost like I wasn't working** – but when I added up the income I had an **extremely successful week** – I actually added up the numbers a few times because I could hardly believe it! But now I am a believer!" – *Sarah Angelli, New York*

"Since doing the deep money monster work and aligning with my higher self-ally/ Money Ally… or Money Honey… **I immediately received new clients and delinquent loan payments to total $8,000.** I continued to do this daily work plus other inner work… and I have received **other money from unexpected** sources that when paid forward will more than make up for my Real Estate losses in retirement funds. **I could feel that the universe was looking for a way to share the abundance**. Thank you so much… for your delicious approach to working with the shadow." – *Lynn Horton*

FINANCIAL ALCHEMY®

Twelve Months of Magic
& Manifestation

MORGANA RAE

A special thanks and acknowledgement go to all my teachers, students, friends and family including Edward Rasch, Darlyne Liddle, Devin Galaudet, Amy Galaudet, Lisa Moore, Michael Stratford, Cat Williford, Chuck Allen, Barbarah Schiffman, Faith Fuller, Marita Fridjhon, Robert Silverstone, Chris Howard, Colleen McGunnigle, Cindie Chavez, Linda Strick, and many, many others.

This book is dedicated to your magic.

We are all magicians.

Cover art by Dan Fowler www.theimaginationinstitute.com

Front Cover Photo by Ulrike Reinhold

Back Cover Photo by Gaelyn Miriam Larrick

www.MorganaRae.com

CONTENTS

Note from the Author

Ten years after releasing my first *Financial Alchemy*® book to far greater acclaim than even I had anticipated (and mountains of subsequent reader success stories, including the client who had her first quarter-of-a-million-dollar sales month *before* she ever spoke with me or hired me… just using my book on her own) I came to the conclusion that this book desperately needed an update to reflect what I know and teach NOW: the new shifts and insights that dramatically multiplied my coaching clients achieving multi-million dollar results over the last decade.

It is the nature of existence to evolve and improve through practice and experience, and this work is no exception. Hence, I created this 10-Year Anniversary Special Edition.

Enjoy, and be sure to let me know if anything interesting happens for you!

INTRODUCTION

Welcome to Financial Alchemy® and the most magical year of your life!

Have you ever noticed how some people work hard, do all the right stuff, and still can't get ahead, while others attract whatever they want effortlessly?

Everyone has magic. Life becomes difficult when you try to do someone else's magic instead of your own. Effortless manifestation is learnable, and the pages ahead of you reflect years of my most successful and most requested secrets for manifestation.

The underlying principles of all magic are intention and inner shift. Set your intention for gentle and effortless shift.

Note the day you begin this program. See yourself a year from now, looking back on the best year of your life!

Part One: Financial Alchemy®

The journey starts with money.

Why money? Money is the #1 excuse I've observed human beings share for what we can't have, do, or be. Let's turn this around and move on!

The Financial Alchemy section of the book will guide you to create a new relationship with money. You will literally make money FALL IN LOVE with you. The remaining exercises will help you anchor your learnings and expand your "Money Honey" abundance consciousness.

Part Two: Magic and Manifestation

Your new year starts any time you begin. This program helps you design the next twelve months and supports you every day along the way. This is where the fairy dust hits the road—you make things happen! Or, rather, you co-create things happening with the universe's assistance. That's the point, isn't it? You get to go farther than you have in the past, and go farther than you could by yourself.

Over the next twelve months, you have the opportunity to master magic and manifestation, create momentum from your own actions, and create space for miracles.

The first step of this magical year is setting your theme. Your theme determines your direction, creates a context for your goals and your decisions, and it sensitizes you to opportunities. A theme looks something like, "play a bigger game," "unstoppable," "fun," "partnership," "expansion," "love," or "appreciation." This will be the filter for your entire life over the next year. For instance, if your theme were "play a bigger game," how might you play a bigger game at home, at work, in your relationships, in health?

Then, from your theme, you set the top priorities for the next twelve months. Parcel your goals quarter by quarter: the point is reducing overwhelm, not trying to do it all at once. Lighten your load. Learn to set priorities. There will come times over the year when all those seeds you planted will spring into full grown oaks at the same moment. A lot will be going on at once. You will rise to that challenge. You don't have to create energetic traffic jams ahead of time.

Every quarter begins with an article to support your progress for that time period.

The weekly journal is the heart of the Magic & Manifestation experience. A year is created by its weeks and days. Every week you will practice clarifying your priorities, choosing your actions, building your wealth, and playing "Ask the universe" for assistance. The weekly journal will help you shift the way you see the world, while every day you will recognize your successes and build your confidence and momentum. It's these little daily habits that will move you forward faster.

This has been an overview of what's to come. The magic and manifestation begin now!

To your adventure, Morgana Rae

PART ONE

Financial Alchemy®

THE SECRET OF
FINANCIAL ALCHEMY®
Create a new relationship with money

Your current financial situation is a direct reflection of your inner relationship with Money. If you don't like your financial experience (money drama can show up whether you have zero or billions), something needs to change in your relationship. This is where Alchemy comes in.

Alchemy is the art of transmuting lead into gold. For my purposes, I'm talking about transmuting leaden human experience into spiritual and material gold. With roots in ancient Egypt and classical Greece, the art of Alchemy arose in a time when there was no distinction between science and magic. The mysteries of matter and consciousness were inextricably linked (as they are again in today's quantum physics). These ancient studies gave birth to modern medicine, psychology, chemistry, and even Sir Isaac Newton's work on gravity.

The ultimate pursuit of Alchemy was the "Philosophers' Stone," a substance believed to turn worthless metals into gold. While Alchemists through the ages slaved in the laboratory, their metalwork concealed a spiritual process, a Philosophers' Stone, which had to be kept hidden from the Church. This was the process of inner transformation. Two principles are involved here: 1) turning lead into gold was an outer demonstration of inner transformation, and 2) the seed of the solution (the gold) was hidden in the problem (the lead).

I invite you to use this chapter to discover your own Philosophers' Stone: your key to wealth and inner transformation—hidden in your relationship with Money.

Before we proceed, let's review some guidelines I adapted from Alchemist tradition:

Rule #1: As it is above, so it is below.

What shows up in your head is going to show up in your life. This chapter will be using fundamental Relationship Coaching skills to help you transform your relationship with money from a dead seed into a flowering garden. A seed comes to life as a living, thriving, fruit-flowering plant...in the right environment. So, too, your own prosperity. Your potential for financial abundance is there, waiting for the necessary environment within you. Your relationship with money is like the soil that feeds or starves your economic growth. As long as you have hidden beliefs that cause you to unconsciously repel money, perhaps "protect" yourself from wealth, your garden will not grow.

Rule #2: There is no scarcity.

A wealthy client once explained to me what he discovered AFTER he had overcome financial poverty: "The amount of money out there in play every day is limitless, beyond our comprehension. Money is everywhere," he explained, "and it's available in proportion to how big your funnel is to allow it in." He had learned to tap into the Source. This relationship supported him.

Rule #3: Consciousness gives you choice.

I assert even a small change in your relationship consciousness can have a huge impact on your material life. You get what you choose, but first you need to know what you're choosing.

How do I know this? I experienced this transformation myself. Then I repeated this transformation with thousands of clients.

My Story

Having proven definitively that a fancy education, celebrity clients, taglines and testimonials, half a dozen master coach certifications, and every Law of Attraction gimmick in the world were no match for my own Superpowers of Money Repulsion, I started my journey struggling to make $100 a month in Los Angeles, California, one of the most expensive cities in the world. I had taken every marketing course, sales course, and mindset course available in the late 90s and early aughts, and I had a reputation for working magic in the entertainment industry. None of it mattered. I was still making $100 a month.

I worked harder. Took more classes. Got more skills. Built up more debt. I had two vision boards (over achiever, right?), a bunch of affirmations, and I went to spiritual healers who would wave their hands in my face and "heal my money DNA."

I was still making $100 a month, and even that was looking sketchy.

I could no longer keep trying. After one too many disappointments, I remember getting on my bed and screaming as I fell down a rabbit hole of rage, despair, and exhaustion. I wanted to leave the planet.

When I cried myself out, I had an odd thought: "What was inside of me that couldn't be with money?" The next day I found out.

I had a call with my coach. (I couldn't afford rent, food, cable, insurance, but I still had a coach?) My coach and I began by examining my relationship with Money… and then the conversation took a weird turn that changed my life forever.

My coach asked, **"If your money were a person, who would your money be?"**

Money, in that moment was a big, scary, dirty, violent biker-dude who terrified me. (Nothing wrong with bikers. This imaginary one was a bad dude.) I could feel every cell of my being screaming for maximum distance between the biker and myself. For the first time in my life, looking at that imaginary biker-dude and observing my own full-body urgency to protect myself from him, my financial situation made perfect sense: No wonder I wasn't bringing money into my life! There was no way I could be with money if it was THIS guy. He was dangerous. This relationship had to end. I made a decision and banished the biker.

I never knew how omnipresent that biker bad-guy money "monster" was until he was gone. I could feel a giant emptiness in the air around me, where he had always been. I knew I needed a new relationship with money to fill that space before that monster returned—nature abhors a vacuum—but I was scared to create more of the same. (If you've ever been in a soul-crushing abusive relationship that made you feel like you weren't good enough, weren't safe, weren't wanted, you know how urgently you do NOT want to land in another relationship like that one.) I could only move forward with something radically different.

New Relationship With Money

I asked myself, "Who could I want in my life so much that I'd be willing to have this person in my life, even if it was money?" As soon as I asked the question, I saw my new money: tall, handsome, clean-cut, romantic. He wore a tuxedo and carried a bouquet of red flowers, as if he were sweeping me off to the opera. He was a sweet boyfriend who wanted to woo me. Can you imagine what it would be like to be wooed by "money"? I related to him in a whole new way. This was the guy I *wanted* to have a relationship with. He loved me. He shared my values. He wanted to be with me.

In that moment, I had an awareness that I had been breaking this lovely being's heart for years, pushing him away. I had the power in the relationship. I had the body. I was the gatekeeper. I also realized I didn't have a clue *how* to let him/money stay with me the way he clearly wanted to.

The great thing about turning money into a person is you can ask a question and get an answer. I asked my new money honey, "What do you need from me so you can stay with me?"

Money responded, "Appreciate me. Love me. Stop treating me like a monster."

I immediately saw how I had been treating him like a monster every time I hesitated to state my fee or didn't demand payment. I vowed to change my behavior. Within 24 hours, 4 people called me up, out of the blue, to hire me as their coach. I picked up four new clients at double the rate I had ever charged before. (The fee I agreed upon with my Money Honey, naturally.) At the time, I could feel my mouth wanting to move in the familiar patterns that would talk clients out of the sale. I had to literally bite my tongue and shut up and let them hire me. You don't say 'no' to gifts from your beloved.

Whenever I received a check, signed a new client, came across some unexpected income, I graciously thanked Money for the gift. I wasn't just thanking an abstract concept of abundance—I was thanking a "person" who was real to me. And this version of Money was valued and invited into my life.

This distinction is important. The primary reason I had been pushing money away (unconsciously) was that I had some time, long ago, made the connection that money got in the way of love. I, like many spiritual healer types, hated charging money because I feared I would be harming someone by "taking" their money. When my focus shifted to being a loving partner to my money person, my relationship to serving my clients shifted, too. I started to recognize that these would-be clients were worthy of a lot more respect than I had been giving them. They were fully formed intelligent adults who could decide for themselves what was harmful or helpful to them, what they should invest in or not. I no longer needed to protect them from my money monster.

My business and income kept growing. Within six months of meeting my money honey, I had accrued such a waiting list of clients that I had to add group coaching to my services. I didn't have to look for my new clients; they were finding me. And it all started by changing my inner relationship with money as a person.

Now it's your turn!

If you want to improve your financial situation, I always like to start with the negative beliefs that shaped your relationship with Money. Get out some paper and respond to these questions. (Writing creates clarity and speeds your change.)

- What negative things have you heard about money?

- What are some of the negative ways money has shown up in your life and in the lives of those around you.

- What beliefs get between you and prosperity?

- Dig deeper and deeper. You may hit several blank spots before you find the deepest beliefs that have truly driven your relationship with money.

But Wait! There's More!

Advanced Alchemy

The money questions above are a great start, and a lot of people have had impressive results going no further.

I also found that client results got dramatically BIGGER when I made an important *shift* in uncovering the root cause before personifying your money monster.

I'm going to teach you *a secret that's going to make this process work shockingly better:* Your relationship with money is never really about money. This is counter-intuitive, but the best way to uncover the root cause of your money monster is to dig into the pains that aren't obviously about money. Money is such a sticky, painful, taboo topic because of what money represents: Love, Worth, Safety, and Power.

Anything in your life that ever made you feel powerless, unloved, unworthy, or unsafe is critically important here. Especially if it doesn't look like it has to do with money. At the end of the day, it has everything to do with money. For example, your parents are your first experience of money. They fed and clothed and sheltered you, just like money. They valued you or they didn't. They loved you or they didn't. They kept you safe or they didn't. They were the gatekeepers to everything you wanted, much like money today. Take a look at accidents, illnesses, violence, heartbreaks, betrayals, and any experience in your life—or in the world at large—that makes the world feel like a dangerous, unkind place.

I call this the first step of Financial Alchemy®: Uncover the Root Cause.

Warning! We are not trying to retraumatize you here. Be gentle. Know your limits. If you feel you're going too far, pull back. You do not need to harm yourself for this process to work. You just need to feel *enough* of what you want in order to produce enough tension (like a slingshot) to make a change of direction inevitable. This process works best when it is experiential, not intellectual. When the world looks and feels bad enough, imagine there's one unique, powerful, sadistic person responsible for all of it, and this person is obsessed with you.

That is your Money Monster.

How big is it? Is it hot or cold? Does it have a gender? What does it smell like? Can you see its hands? Its eyes? Its teeth? Catch a whiff of its breath. What does it say to itself when it looks at you? What does it want to do to you? Think of the meanest thing you've ever said to yourself. Now imagine it was your monster whispering into your ear, in your voice.

This is the second step of Financial Alchemy®: Personify the Root Cause.

If this monster is your relationship with money, do your financial challenges make more sense now?

The more real and human this monster is, the better. Your money monster embodies *everything* you do not want in your life experience. Whether it's personal stuff or global stuff (animal abuse, climate change, human trafficking, racism, misogyny... whatever's your hot button issue), this is your moment to REJECT what you do not want. Only one of you gets to survive. Choose yourself and slay your monster. By any means necessary. (This is your imagination. You have no limits.)

End that relationship, baby! And leave no bloody bits.

When the monster is completely gone, **feel the difference**. You may feel exhilarated or you may feel a little fear or grief; both are perfect. All that matters is you feel *different*. A difference you've never felt before.

Yay you! You Slayed the beast!

You have completed the third step of Financial Alchemy®: Obliterate your Money Monster.

Are you ready for the fun part? (Yes, there is a fun part!) Now you get to meet your new relationship with money, your "money honey."

After you've annihilated your "money" monster and rejected everything that does not belong in your life experience, all that remains is love. Your new relationship will feel like love, not cash.

Quick tip for meeting your money honey: pick a location. Imagine to yourself where you'd like to meet your beloved for the first time. Feel what you feel, see what you see, hear what you hear in this location. Now imagine your money honey is walking towards you.

Here are the rules of your new relationship: This person lights you up. This person adores you. This person chooses you over everyone in the world. You want this relationship because you want to be with this person, not because this person is "money."

(FYI: If you're married and turned on and worried that you're cheating on your spouse... Congratulations!!!! You just hit a home run! No, you are not cheating on your human honey with your imaginary friend. Bravo to you for successfully conjuring a relationship so real and delicious that you had that concern. Bring that erotic energy to your human partner. They'll appreciate it!)

Meeting your Money Honey is Step Four of Financial Alchemy®

You're almost at the finish line. You uncovered the root cause of your toxic relationship with money. You slayed your money monster. You met your money honey. Only two more steps to complete the process.

- Dialogue your money honey. What does Money need from you to stay with you? This is also a great time to just cuddle with your money person and take a look at your life circumstances as a team. What does your money honey see differently?

This is Step Five of Financial Alchemy®

- Commit to action. Action is magical. When you want tangible real-world results, taking tangible-real world action helps bring the shift down from the ether and into physical reality. Negotiate with your new money honey. What concrete, measurable action can you take to demonstrate to Money and yourself that this relationship has changed? Check in and see how your partner responds. Is the response "Meh?" or "Okay, but more?" or "Yesssss! This!!!!" That's how you know.

This is Step Six, the final step of Financial Alchemy®

Do what you say you'll do. Keep your word. The more trustworthy you are, the more deserving you will feel. You will find yourself being more attractive to Money and everything else you desire.

Money is like any other relationship: It comes where it's invited and appreciated. It rarely comes when it is chased. It can be your partner if you listen to it. The more you care for this relationship, the more this partnership will flourish.

Here are three final tips:

1) Appreciate money! When a penny shows up on the sidewalk, thank Money for the gift. Don't worry about denomination; appreciate everything. Think of how good you feel when you are valued for even a small gesture. It's the same for Money. Every time you practice receiving and appreciating, you train the universe to send you more. Show the universe what you value.

2) By now your capacity to receive is growing. You'll notice other stuff creeps in to limit the flow through your funnel to abundance. This stuff may look like clutter, broken appliances, old e-mails, toxic people, time wasters or other energy drains. Clean house! Make space for what you want by having the courage to release what you don't want. You teach the universe how you want to be treated with every choice you make. And nothing gets the universe's attention like saying "No." It's your quickest ticket to miracles.

3) The most important place to make space for what you want is in your head. Clean out fear and pessimism. Plant love and trust instead. Your thoughts are your seeds, and you can grow flowers or weeds. What do you choose to grow?

And to make the process work even better...

SPECIAL GIFT
FOR YOU!

My life passion is to help people be the success they dream about, and I want to give you every advantage in creating a quick breakthrough.

I believe in rewarding commitment.

You've come this far, and that's why I've arranged a **FREE BONUS mp3** download for you of my most popular audio class, "Be Irresistibly Magnetic to Money."

This recording will help you dig deeper into the process to help you make your NEW relationship with money that much more real, alive, and powerful for you.

Go here: www.MoneyMagnetGift.com to get your "Be Irresistibly Magnetic to Money" audio download.

JOHN TRAVOLTA LOVES YOU

Let's take a step away from all this money relationship theory and take a look at Alchemy in Action.

This story came in from a Financial Alchemist named Lynn Swanson. Not only does she tell a great tale—with humor, drama, and a spooky miracle at the end— she illustrates some pieces of the process that will make the same kind of transformation easier for you.

Read Lynn's tale of Financial Alchemy® in her life, and I'll share the secret lessons at the end:

> "Hi Morgana—Hope this is not too long…just had to share!
>
> Last night, I asked my Money Honey what I should do to have more of him in my life. He showed up dressed like John Travolta in the *Saturday Night Fever* white suit. I couldn't figure out what was going on…but each time I tried to picture him in different clothes, he changed back into the white suit. So, I gave up and let him dress as he pleased.
>
> Anyway, he told me that the next thing to do was to go to the bank in the morning, and deposit some money from one of my checking accounts to the other. I thought, "OK." And thanked him for stopping by…said 'adios.'
>
> We have been struggling to collect money from many of our clients right now, and I was feeling a little panicked because I didn't have enough funds to cover our payroll due to our employees on Friday. We had been contacting our clients who were 'past due,' but hadn't been making any progress. So…this morning, at about 10:20, I left work to go to the bank. I put the deposit into the ATM machine, and walked back to my car.
>
> Turned on the car, and SATURDAY NIGHT FEVER was playing on the radio. At first it didn't 'click' with me, but then all of a sudden, I started laughing out loud, I thought, "what a synchronicity"!
>
> Then, I went to order a coffee for an employee that I had promised to pick up on my way back. As I was waiting for the coffee, I got an email from one of our clients. They were paying us EARLY on a project we just invoiced for! (five figures) They were paying the SAME DAY that we invoiced and were over-nighting the check!
>
> The amount of the check WILL EASILY COVER OUR PAYROLL—and the money wasn't due to us for 45 MORE DAYS!!
>
> The time on my deposit slip is 10:35 AM; the time the client emailed me to tell me about the early payment is 10:37 AM.!! TWO MINUTES!!

I still can't believe it—I'm in awe.

Thanks for sharing this powerful tool with me. I am forever appreciative."

Pretty wild, huh?

Here were some clues that let me know the process was working even before we got to the big five-figure punchline at the end of the story.

1) Her new relationship with Money (her "Money Honey") showed up with a personality of his own. She didn't create him: he was already made! Do you hear how he "just showed up"? Perfect!

2) This points to one of the most important things you need to understand about your Money Honey: He ALREADY EXISTS, and he CHOOSES YOU over anybody else in the world. He's your relationship with Money, and the polar opposite of your rejecting monster.

3) Her money has a sense of humor. First, the John Travolta costume, then the music.

4) Lynn took action even when his direction (move cash from one account to another? Whatever!) didn't make obvious sense. She got out of her head and into the relationship, and she followed through. She did it anyway.

The big check is a marvelous confirmation that the process worked, but the real transformation happened BEFORE the cash arrived. See?

SUSTAINING YOUR NEW RELATIONSHIP

You can't just tell your partner "I love you" and be good to go for the next twenty years. Your relationship with Money is as real and dynamic as your relationship with another human being. You have to stay in communication.

If you don't pay attention to your Money Honey, you'll see the results in your bank account. That's how Money wakes you up and gets you back into the relationship.

As with all relationships, it's not always smooth sailing. Stuff happens. You freak out. You blame Money.

You can practice the Law of Attraction all you like, and you'll still hit setbacks. Your computer crashes, you lose clients, or the job ends. That's life.

At those moments of challenge, you have a choice: Do you stay in this relationship or not? How committed are you? Are you willing to stay in the game when Money makes you mad?

These rough patches can be the best opportunities to learn something new, deepen your relationship, and discover new ways to manifest abundance. Sometimes Money expresses love by challenging you to be bigger and more creative than you see yourself.

Next time you feel stressed about your finances, here are a few things you can do:

1) Talk to Money. Say, "I'm feeling anxious, Money. What do you want me to do so I can feel less anxious?" Then do it.

2) Make a list of twenty ways you can make money quickly. This exercise will take you back to your creativity, resourcefulness, and power.

3) Be grateful. Thank Money for having always been there for you. If you're alive and reading this book today, you've had the food, shelter, and resources to be here now. Money has always been there for you.

Don't wait until you have a financial crisis to talk to Money. I encourage you to keep asking your Money, "What do you want from me to make you happy?"

"What do you need from me so you can stay with me?"

The answer that comes back to you may surprise you. Frequently, Money will tell you things that have nothing to do with your finances. Money may say things like, "play more," or "clean your house," or "exercise," or "improve your relationship with your spouse." It's all connected. Self-care is very attractive to wealth.

Your communication takes practice. Sometimes you'll get your answers loud and clear. Other times the response is so quick and quiet that you can pretend you didn't hear it.

You can take Money with you on job interviews, dates, or any uncomfortable situation. When in doubt, ask your Money Honey for guidance. You make Money happy when you value yourself, but boy do you make Money angry when you disrespect yourself!

I set my fees according to what will make Money feel loved and honored. We have a conversation. We negotiate what I charge. He feels I'm worth x amount. I feel comfortable charging y. We usually come to an agreement somewhere in between, and I stick to that amount. My fee isn't based on how I feel about myself on any given day. I charge what I charge because I want to be a good relationship partner. I'm demonstrating that I value my Money sweetheart. I feel like I'm cheating on him when I cut my rates.

You're going to have a relationship with Money until the day you die, so you better make it a good one. The quality of your relationship is entirely up to you. You are in the power seat. Money depends on you to be a loving partner, even when you don't want to be, so you can manifest a truly abundant life.

Quick Tip: Change Happens at the Speed of Safety

After coaching thousands of clients over three decades, I noticed this pattern: If you've been doing everything you can to solve a problem or change your situation—in money, love, health, whatever—and you aren't seeing the results you deserve, you are NOT a loser or a failure. You are not a self-saboteur. You are, in fact, very *successful* at protecting yourself from an existential threat. The threat is real. Your conscious awareness may not see it, but your unconscious mind has kept a perfect record of every hurt, disappointment, and danger embedded in your goal.

Stuckness is self-protection. I have found it to be far more useful to have appreciation and gratitude for this protection strategy than judgment and contempt. When we can see stuckness for what it is—self-defense—then we can create better strategies for safety. When being stuck no longer serves a purpose, it has a very strong tendency to disappear.

The results you desire can come in very fast when you've successfully made what you want safe. I've noticed the results can be far bigger than you imagined for yourself. It's as if all those years of effort have built an energetic backlog for what you want coming to you.

Next time you find yourself feeling stuck and frustrated, take a pause and choose compassion for yourself. What might be the hidden fears and dangers lurking behind your dream?

Slay a new Money Monster. Or maybe this time it's a Love Monster. (I met my husband two months after slaying my Love Monster.) Or come up with any monster that's in your way.

Then take a fresh look at how to get what you want in partnership with your new, safe, "Honey" on the other side.

Extra Bonus: scan the QR code below on your smartphone for bonus video content or go to https://www.morganarae.com/pCG50!

MONEY LIKES AND DISLIKES

If you're going to make Money a person, "Money" is going to, well, have a *personality*.

And that personality has some quirks.

Over the years, I've noticed that client "Money Honeys" (that new, wonderful relationship with a money who LOVES you!) tend to certain predispositions.

In other words, Money just likes some stuff and doesn't like other stuff. Here's a rundown of the most common Money Honey likes and dislikes:

Money Likes

- Fun

- Sexy lingerie (Money keeps sending my clients shopping)

- Dancing

- Animals and pets (especially dogs, horses, and fluffy red cats)

- Attention

- Appreciation

- Self-worth

- Self-confidence

- Romance

- Flowers

- Strong personal boundaries

- Quality

- Talks in the car (Money likes to sit in the passenger seat)

- Love

- Trust

- France (whether it's trips to Paris or French cuisine, your Money Honey digs France!)

Money Dislikes

- Being rejected and blamed

- Clutter

- Fast food

- Shabbiness

- Undercharging

- Overcharging

- People pleasing

- Cruelty to animals

- Cheating

- Junk/buying crap (if you're going to spend, make it count)

- Disorder and disregard

- Not standing up for yourself

- Ugly clothing (it's really not attractive)

- Pollution

- Waste

- Complacency

- Too-small hotel rooms (My Money Honey complained to me, years ago on a trip to Melbourne, Australia, that our room was too small. "I can't believe you dragged me across the planet for this! Have you no sense of romance?" he protested. I changed rooms immediately!)

HOT, SEXY, AND READY FOR A TUMBLE

Why is imagining Money as a hot, sexy, super-lover so powerful? (We're talking windfalls of hundreds, thousands, even tens of thousands of dollars within hours of creating a new relationship.) Making Money a best friend, a doting grandparent, a faerie, or Oprah just doesn't cut it.

Here's why this works:

- The stakes are higher when sex is involved. It's in our DNA. Grandma's house or a slumber party with Idris Alba? You decide.
- The relationship is more equal: Our lover wants reciprocation. Everybody thinks, "What has Money done for me lately?" Not many people ask, "How can I make Money happy?" It's a world of difference and the key to dramatic results.
- A man will do ANYTHING to win the woman he loves. Just watch a guy drunk dial.
- Ditto for women.

Napoleon Hill, the author of *Think and Grow Rich*, figured this out and alludes to it in his chapter on the "Mystery of Sex Transmutation." (This is the chapter most people ignore!) Napoleon got it right: Sex Transmutation is the foundation of the most powerful magic.

Napoleon rated the ten great motivators of human behavior from the "highest rates of vibration" to the lowest. They are:

1) The desire for sex expression. (That's us!)

2) Love.

3) A burning desire for fame, power, financial gain, money.

4) Music. (This one surprised me. When you think about it, music works on a deeper level than the conscious mind.)

5) Friendship.

6) A Master Mind alliance.

7) Mutual suffering.

8) Autosuggestion.

9) Fear.

10) Addiction.

We spend most of our time in our heads, and that works great up to a point. We spend a little bit of time in our hearts, and perhaps we get truer information there. Real action and attraction come from the groin. That fluffy faerie crown chakra stuff is all well and good, but creation comes from sex. You won't feel anything stronger or deeper... so to speak.

PS: I've had a couple of clients try to create a new relationship with Money by imagining Money as a unicorn. Not a good idea. The results were miserable. You can't **** a unicorn.

PPS: For those of you who are worried you'll be cheating on your spouse, that is an excellent sign that your new Money is real to you. Perfect! This is what we want! I can absolutely PROMISE you that you will never sleep with your imaginary friend. In fact, the confidence and desire your new Money brings out in you can be *fantastic* for your marriage!

PPPS: If you have suffered sexual abuse in the past, your sexuality may be so wrapped up in your old Money Monster that creating a sexy Money Honey feels unsafe. That's okay. Your new Money will respect the boundaries of what is safe and comfortable for you. He will never force you. He will hold you to the exact extent at which you'll feel protected, loved and honored. Let him help you heal the old wounds.

> *"I listened to your audio class and had a deeply powerful healing experience of breaking up with the money monster — and deeply committing to money honey. I realized I have been afraid to say, 'I Love You!' to money. It opened up my whole world to say it — to really acknowledge that I love money and my honey was deeply relieved and said he had been really wanting to hear that and was so happy that I finally said it — because it was the first time I had. So, we are doing very well, and I am enjoying being in a real relationship with money."* — Sarah Angelli
>
> REMEMBER! *Access your BONUS AUDIO CLASS at www.MoneyMagnerGift.com*

MONEY HONEY OF THE HIGHLANDS

Let's be candid for second: Is your "new" relationship with money real? Or is it a shallow, warmed-over monster who looks good in jeans? Or have you been struggling to get a clear picture of your personified "Money Honey," but it's not quite there?

Welcome to the land of FAKE MONEY HONEYS. Sorry kids. You haven't *really* gotten there yet.

I received a SWOON WORTHY account of romance with a true Money Honey. This is what Financial Alchemy really looks like. Accept no substitute.

This is from a long email, utterly delicious, from Financial Alchemist Rush Cole. As you read her Money Honey encounter, I want you to notice the contrast between the seriousness of her past—the tragic circumstances that created her Money Monster—and the joyous whimsy of her new relationship, and how it changes her WHOLE life. And the real lessons she learns about money and love in the end. Cash is just the tip of the iceberg…

"Early last April," Rush writes, "one of your coaches introduced me to you and your teachings about changing one's relationship with money. I felt the truth in it and immediately set about getting rid of my personal 'money monster.' And boy, did I have a doozie of one!

My childhood had been spent in a private war zone masquerading as the all-American family. By the time I was twelve, I'd been repeatedly beaten, burned, stabbed, and abused in every way by the two people I should have been able to trust and depend upon to love me and want only the best for me. In addition to stealing my Self and my Innocence, they also stole my car and my money before throwing me out into the world with only the clothes on my back. I've worked the past two decades to heal my Self and to live Whole.

A few years ago, I began realizing that I'd succeeded pretty well to the point where I found myself saying with increasing frequency, 'Gee, you know, everything in my life is just getting better and better , and I'm so happy these days. The only thing missing is money; I just wish I could stabilize my money situation.'

Your approach to money, Morgana, and allowing oneself to have a passionately loving relationship with a personal Money Honey touched and excited me. Suddenly, I wanted such a relationship with all of my heart. So, I promptly called in my Money Honey and married him on April 18th.

Amazingly, things went downhill from there. When cash did come to me, it was always a 'day late and a dollar short.' I found myself borrowing against money that I was supposed to receive but was somehow always delayed. Finally, I realized that my Money Honey was someone who'd been with me for as long as I could remember.

He wasn't a monster at all, he'd been victimized along with me, and I had no clue about how to heal his wounds, too. So, I divorced him on November 4, and sent him, with love, down his own path with a prayer for his total healing.

The next morning, I awoke early to the realization that there was a new man in my mind's eye, a braw-laddie of a man, full-grown, wickedly handsome and looking at me as if he were starving and I the last morsel of food on earth! I'm telling you, Morgana, my blood heated at the mere sight of him, and I blushed, even as I told myself that I'd gone 'round the bend' for sure this time! Here I was, alone in my bed, feeling all beside myself because I'm imagining there's an awesomely masculine man in my bedroom, flirting with me and it's not even six a.m. yet.

Just as I'm throwing back the covers and getting out of bed, he steps out of the way and volunteers that his name is Duncan. At the same moment, I realize that he's wearing a kilt and that he's got fabulous legs, all strong and bronzed. He snorted with laughter, and I blushed again, thinking that my boyfriend wouldn't be amused to know I was experiencing such a vivid early morning daydream about an imaginary man.

'I'm not imaginary, Darlin,' I'm your "real" Money Honey,' Duncan spoke up, startling me.

'You? But how can that be? I just sent the other one away last night.'

'Well,' Duncan responded, his grey eyes gleaming at me, 'I've been watchin' ye for a while, ever since ye connected with Morgana. Ye weren't ready for me last April, so I've just been waiting for ye to come to your own conclusions and make new choices.'

'But who are you?' I whispered, feeling my heart open and my whole being yearn toward this man of my dreams. In that instant, I really looked at him and knew that it was him I'd been missing all of my adult life.

Duncan nodded, knowing I needed details. 'I'm a Scottish Laird from a long, long line of the same. I was born into wealth and taught, as was me father before me, how to protect our wealth, how to grow it so that the next laird of our clan has even more than I do. Och, and it's not as if I'm lacking anything material, lass; I never have and I never will. I've no notion of lack in my consciousness, just the desire to teach you all that I know about treating your Money as if he's the most perfect lover you've ever imagined. Lucky for me, I'm your Money, Honey!'

Whether I believe he's real, or not, whether I can logically explain Duncan Macrae's existence in my life to anyone else, I know that he has come through Time and Space to teach and help me with this last huge, personal wound of mine. Most of all, Duncan Macrae has chosen to personify my Money Honey, *to show me experientially how it feels to be loved totally, unconditionally, in every way.* He is definitely NOT here to rescue me; my Money is teaching me to rescue myself.

I've begun referring to my financial wealth as simply "cash"; I no longer equate it with my Money Honey.

What he is constantly giving to me is fine and rare, pure and precious, that I feel as if I am living the most wonderful dream I could ever have.

Duncan compliments me often, helps me gain clarity when I'm confused, especially about finances, and has a wondrously magical sense of humor. He'll whisper to me to turn on the radio in my truck at the exact moment a song by Craig Morgan begins to play. A delivery truck with the name "Morgan" painted on it came up alongside me on the interstate one afternoon. When I glanced over at it, the dark-haired, silver-eyed hottie of a driver smiled at me and winked!

Right, like I don't know that Duncan is reminding me that he's all part and parcel of what you've been telling all of us is true, Morgana: Our Money Honey is not about how much cash we possess.

> *True wealth is the sense of profound wellbeing that comes with knowing that we are loved for ourselves, just as we are.*

Money truly is what I've always missed and yearned for and craved, but it's not about just cash, not anymore. I am in love with my Money Honey, totally, irrevocably, joyfully. The sense of existential loneliness I had learned to accept as the way of life is rapidly diminishing and Life feels new these days.

One last note: I don't feel any guilt at all about loving Duncan Macrae so passionately. My boyfriend of five years knows nothing about Morgana or my Money Honey, not consciously, that is. What he does know, though, is that I am changing, becoming stronger and surer and even more attractive to him. He may not know the reason for the changes, but he is also much more attentive and loving to me nowadays.

I tell myself, at least a dozen times a day, that I am living the life of my dreams, filled with all the beauty and joy and love that I've found and created for myself. And now, I have Money, too!

Blessed Be, Morgana, I am so glad that you and I are in the world at the same time! Thank you for sharing your gift."

Rush Cole, Santa Fe
www.rushcolefineart.com

THE FINANCIAL ALCHEMY PROCESS DEMONSTRATED

You've read my story, but what does the transformation process actually look like with someone else? Below is a transcript of a live coaching demonstration, illustrating the whole Financial Alchemy process from beginning to end, from old money to new. (The client's name has been changed.)

Maria:	I have a holistic practice with a few clients. I've done a lot of training. I've come up with a lot of fear around money and wanting to hold on to it.
	There is the feeling that I should put God first. How do I balance that? I'm supposed to be spiritual, so I shouldn't be so fearful about money.
Morgana:	I know where you're coming from. Why don't you tell me some of the negative things you've heard or observed about money? Give it to me.
Maria:	Growing up, I lived with my father and grandfather. We had an extended family. There would be physical fights over money, even if my grandfather bought two loaves of bread. It was constant. It was like money was God.
	Money was power and control. Part of me sees that. Part of me feels like I need to have a man to be able to have money. I don't have a man in my life.
	There were tremendous daily fights. They weren't always physical, but it happened. It was really frightening.
	I was considered cheap. I would put my little paychecks in the bank. I would want to round up my money to receive change to do that. There were feelings of shame about how much I wanted money.
Morgana:	We'll dig a little bit, but we have to go quickly. What I'm hearing so far is that money causes fights and violence. It's controlling and frightening. You feel cheap. It causes shame.
	This is your money monster.
	This is the guy who causes the fights, commits the violence and is controlling and frightening. He's cheap on top of that!

He causes you shame. It almost sounds to me like he's holding you hostage. This is a violent, scary guy.

Maria: There was a woman we hired to help out when my grandmother was in the hospital. I had no mother. I felt betrayed because she stole money out of our piggy banks. I thought she liked me.

Morgana: That's horrible.

Maria: When you were talking, I had a remembrance of that. It's been years since that happened.

Morgana: Anything else?

Maria: The feeling of not having enough, and yet there are so many poor people. I'm so fortunate to be in the U.S. How dare I want more? Here I am educated, and yet I'm so in debt.

Morgana: You feel undeserving. At the same time, it's not fair that you're in debt. You feel you don't have enough. I don't know if you've ever had a withholding boyfriend or relationship that always made you earn it and only gave you a little bit?

I also heard that you need money from a man. Money is more generous with men than women... so your money is also a misogynist! Are you getting the picture here? It causes fights and violence. It may have only happened once or twice, but that's enough.

It's controlling, manipulative, frightening, and cheap. It feeds off of your shame. It causes betrayal. It doesn't give you enough. It only lets you have so much. It tells you that you're undeserving; you're taking it away from somebody else.

That's a real jerk! I wouldn't want that person in my life. I think you'd be crazy to want to be with that.

Let's imagine this money is a person. Go down to Central Casting. With all of those negative qualities you described, is this money male or female?

Maria: Male. It's a creature. It's goopy. Instead of hands, it has knives.

Morgana: That's scary. How does he make you feel?

Maria: Afraid, like I want to run away. I'm afraid to run away.

Morgana: Sure, because you need to have him in your life whether you want him or not. Do you see how this might possibly be impacting how you're behaving with money and your financial reality?

Maria: Yes. I heard what you said about coming up with a more positive image, something that really feels nurturing and generous.

Morgana: First we put all the nasty stuff into this money villain. That creates the groundwork for the next step. Is this guy with the knife hands tall or short? What color hair? What does he smell like?

Maria: He's stocky and tall. He's grayish-green like stucco. He smells like rotten flesh.

Morgana: Okay, send him off. Do you want him around? Send him off.

You have a clean slate. You can make up whatever you want. You get it.

Maria: I want a Prince Charming.

Morgana: What does he look like?

Maria: He's tall. He's blond and reminds me a little bit of Jesus. He's compassionate and friendly. He loves life.

Morgana: How do you feel about him?

Maria: Grateful.

Morgana: Let's dial up the passion a little bit. What would make him really exciting to you?

Maria: I guess if he was more fun-loving than compassionate. He's adventurous. He's more spontaneous to help me be more like that. He is a multi-billionaire.

Morgana: He won't rescue you. He'll love you. He'll work with you. I want it clear that he won't rescue you.

Maria: I won't get any money?

Morgana: I didn't say that. I said that you have equal power in the relationship. He will not rescue you from yourself. He wants to be loved, too. That's why I want somebody who turns you on. If he looks like Jesus, make him a hot and sexy Jesus.

Maria:	I go for Latin types in that quarter. He'd be dark haired with big brown eyes. He has a nice smile. That's hot.
Morgana:	You want him in your life?
Maria:	Yes!
Morgana:	Bring him in the room and ask him, "Money, what do you need from me so that you can stay with me, the way you really want to?" That's the trick, because he's this hot guy, but he's also *money*.
Maria:	Money, what do you need from me? Do you want to stay with me?
Morgana:	What does he need, in order to stay with you?
Maria:	He said to love and respect him.
Morgana:	Great! What action can you take immediately to show him that you will love and respect him? What will you do to show him—and yourself—that you are committed to this new relationship?
Maria:	I have to balance my checkbook and get my taxes done.
Morgana:	When will you have it done?
Maria:	I'll do it by next Friday.
Morgana:	Ask him how he feels about that.
Maria: do it."	He said "Good." He said, "Don't promise if you won't
Morgana:	That's very important. Will you do it, or do you need to offer something different? Let me tell you, if you don't do it, you will make him feel unwanted, and you will make yourself feel unworthy. Make a commitment you will keep and see how it makes him feel.
Maria:	I'll balance the checkbook.
Morgana:	When you told him you will do it, how did he feel?
Maria:	He said, "I'll believe it when I see it."
Morgana:	Then you know what you have to do.
Maria:	I need to do it.

Morgana: It also sounds like you have to rebuild some trust in this relationship.

Maria: I see it in my relationships. That is my problem with promises, especially to me.

Morgana: You need to create the trust and then you'll be able to trust him better. You will also trust and value yourself more, too. Do you see how that works?

Maria: I have it.

Morgana: Thank you so much for stepping up to the plate.

WHY AFFIRMATIONS ARE PATHETIC

I shouldn't be writing this. Wealth affirmations are such big business for my friends and colleagues and the people who hire me. And affirmations are stupid.

Why?

When you can't get (or leave) a job, or pay your mortgage, or find a date, chanting to yourself, "I'm a millionaire," isn't going to solve your problems.

Affirmations are like putting pretty makeup on a zit. They don't fix anything.

People ask me all the time, "How can I stop having negative thoughts?" You can't. The thoughts aren't the problem; they're the *symptom*.

When I have my first session with a client, I say, "Go for the negative thoughts! Let's really find out what's there." Not just the stuff you know you think about Money/Love/Yourself, but the stuff you had NO IDEA you thought or believed. That's where the magic resides in that: **"Oh my God, I never made that connection before!"** stuff that you feel from the top of your head down to the tips of your toes.

This is *Alchemy*. We create a POLARITY that acts like a slingshot that propels you from one world to the next. THERE'S NO MAGIC IN NEUTRALITY.

When we bring all that to light and *exorcise* your Money Monster with Financial Alchemy, that's when we can move into love, gratitude and vision and have them *mean* something.

If you have some cancerous inner dynamic that is feeding on your personal power, your self-esteem, your relationships and your business—**this is what a bad relationship with Money will do**—the last thing you need is a simple aspirin.

Don't "feel better" without correcting the underlying cause. You may take a couple steps forward, and then find yourself back in the ER. That's where affirmations fall short. They don't address the underlying cause.

It's time to open you up and suck out the poison! When your relationship with Money (which ALWAYS affects your relationships with family, partners, self-worth, and empowerment), transmutes to **a deep, committed, deliriously happy marriage**, then any affirmation dressing you put on top of it will be magical.

I like to use the snake venom metaphor: **Suck out the venom BEFORE you put on the band aid,** (the affirmation). Think of what happens when you put the band aid on before you remove the poison: The poison can't release, and it goes deeper and deeper into your bloodstream. You can watch a black line of poisoned blood creeping from the site of the wound to your heart itself, where it will eventually kill you.

Affirmations are great. They're also useless, worthless, pathetic, and worse if that's as far as you go. It's nice and safe (and lazy) to think that happy thoughts are all the universe wants of you to reach your goals. Frankly I don't know how high you can "vibrate" if you're carrying <u>a lead weight of unacknowledged rage, shame, fear, and hurt</u> behind the velvet curtain of your conscious mind.

There's a big difference between "I want to believe this" and "I DO believe this!" You have to do the real work. I don't think an inner change has to take a long time. Inner change can happen in an instant. (In fact, if you haven't experienced a PROFOUND shift in your very first session, you have the wrong coach!) But you have to do the work and really want a change. <u>That's how you make an affirmation mean something—you</u> <u>are affirming the change that has already happened.</u>

FINANCIAL ALCHEMY®
AFFIRMATIONS

After you've shifted the underlying relationship
with Money, these affirmations rock!

Charmed Life Coaching

Money speaks to me and guides me
to my highest good.

My prosperity serves the world.

People love to give me money because
I add value to their lives.

I respect and appreciate the abundance in my life.

I am wealthy NOW!

APPRECIATION LIST 100

This is where the fun begins! Come up with at least 100 things you are grateful for right now! Acknowledge the gifts that are already in your life. Every time you fall into feelings of lack or fear, writing a gratitude list will return you to your power and possibility. Appreciation is attractive to Money. Start now.

1	26	51	76
2	27	52	77
3	28	53	78
4	29	54	79
5	30	55	80
6	31	56	81
7	32	57	82
8	33	58	83
9	34	59	84
10	35	60	85
11	36	61	86
12	37	62	87
13	38	63	88
14	39	64	89
15	40	65	90
16	41	66	91
17	42	67	92
18	43	68	93
19	44	69	94
20	45	70	95
21	46	71	96
22	47	72	97
23	48	73	98
24	49	74	99
25	50	75	100

WISH LIST 100

Now go shopping for your dreams. Come up with 100 things you would like to be, do, or have. Imagine you get to have everything you want! What's that like for you? See it already accomplished. This game helps you grow your ability to manifest opportunities and fulfill your wishes.

1	26	51	76
2	27	52	77
3	28	53	78
4	29	54	79
5	30	55	80
6	31	56	81
7	32	57	82
8	33	58	83
9	34	59	84
10	35	60	85
11	36	61	86
12	37	62	87
13	38	63	88
14	39	64	89
15	40	65	90
16	41	66	91
17	42	67	92
18	43	68	93
19	44	69	94
20	45	70	95
21	46	71	96
22	47	72	97
23	48	73	98
24	49	74	99
25	50	75	100

NOTES

PART TWO

Magic & Manifestation

TOP FIVE SECRETS OF MAGIC AND MANIFESTATION

"When you really want something to happen, the whole universe conspires so that your wish comes true." ~ The Alchemist, by Paolo Coelho

Manifestation is what you create with your own hands. "Manifest," quite literally, means "gripped by the hand," (manus–hand, festus–gripped).

Magic and Manifestation together are the marriage of your actions and the universe's assistance, the fuel and the fire.

These five secrets will grow your capacity to make your dreams come true:

1. Set inspired, aligned goals.

If you're not reaching a goal, take a look at your goal. How do you know this is right for you at this time? Use your intuition instead of your ego. Find that inspired, joyful place in yourself, and ask what it wants to happen this year, what you're meant to achieve. Allow your answers to come back to you and see that anything you take on feels right and supports where you desire to go in the long term. Trust your source of aligned, inspired wisdom to guide you to goals that fulfill themselves.

2. Underpromise, Overdeliver.

Most people overestimate what they can accomplish in the short term and underestimate what they can accomplish in the long term. If you always promise less than you can do, you can always give more than you promise. Wouldn't you like to be known as, (and know yourself as), the person who follows through and then some? Give your results more time to happen. Take smaller steps. Rack up your wins. Build your confidence, integrity, and momentum. These are very attractive qualities.

3. Focus on the progress instead of the gap.

Do you ever psych yourself out with all the stuff you haven't accomplished? You can make yourself a winner or loser by where you put your focus. The more you focus on lack, the more lack you will see. The more you focus on abundance, accomplishment, and magic, the more they will appear in your life. Human beings have amnesia. Studies have shown that we naturally remember the bad stuff more easily than the good stuff.

Counteract that amnesia. Keep daily records of your successes. Give yourself credit for at least five good things a day. When you feel scared or scarce, make a list of what you're grateful for. When you plan for the next year, make a comprehensive list of all you accomplished the year before.

4. Cut down your "must do" list.

Put things off and cut things out. Too much stuff creates overwhelm and overwhelm can stop you in your tracks. So, set your priorities for the next three months. Anything that can be done six months or nine months from now should be scheduled for later in the year. Focus on what is here now and know that the other stuff will be done in its designated time. And do less.

This is the 80/20 rule: 80% of what you do yields 20% of your results. 20% yields you 80% of the results. Identify your highest impact activities and put those first! Look at what you can delete or delegate from the rest.

5. Partner with the universe.

The whole idea behind Magic and Manifestation is Partnership: you don't have to do it all on your own. There's your job, and there's the universe's job. Your job is what you can control—your actions, your mindset, your game plan. Anything that is outside of your control is the universe's job. Let it go. Focus on your job.

First, you set the goals that are within your control, are easy or manageable. Then you play: set a goal that is just outside your control. Every week, ask for the universe's help in one thing. Start small. (Practice on getting top-notch parking spaces.) Make your request, let it go, and see what happens. It's a game.

As time goes on, you'll see more and more of these requests coming to past. You'll find thoughts like, "I'd like to," or "It would be nice if," bringing those opportunities to you. Then you step back into your job: accept the opportunity and do what needs to be done or decline it and do what needs to be done. And thank the universe for playing!

These are the five secrets to transforming your ability to make the things you want happen in your life. As you put them into practice, pay attention to the following:

1) What's working?

2) What gets in the way?

3) When are you most magical?

Discover your own secrets!

SIR GAWAIN AND THE LOATHSOME LADY

Any instruction manual on magic should include a fairy tale, and what better setting than King Arthur's court?

Once upon a time, long, long ago, King Arthur was riding with his best knight Gawain when they came to the rescue of a damsel in distress. King Arthur fought to free the lady from a black knight with supernatural powers. And he lost. The black knight spared King Arthur's life at the behest of the witch he served. The witch offered to spare King Arthur's life if he could answer her question within one year's time: "What do women want most?"

What do women want most? Sir Gawain and King Arthur puzzled over the question as they returned to Camelot. They questioned their ladies at court, their maids, women of neighboring towns, the countryside, and all the wisest people they could gather. Every one offered a different answer: Money. Love. Power. Beauty. Wealth. Youth. Castles. Servants. Children. Great Sex. Thin thighs. Pierce Brosnan.

The year passed without bringing King Arthur any closer to answering the riddle. And so it was with heavy heart that King Arthur and Sir Gawain returned to meet death at the castle of the black knight, one year after the riddle was posed. Along their journey, a repulsive old hag stepped into their path and wouldn't let them pass. This loathsome lady was the most revolting creature either had seen: she farted and belched; she had a face spotted with hairy moles, broken brown teeth, bloodshot watery eyes, matted, greasy hair that had never been washed, and she had a short and twisted body with lumps and bulges in alarming places.

"I have the answer you seek," she hissed.

"Who are you?" Gawain queried. "What answer?"

"What women want. I am Ragnell, and I will save the king's life for a price."

"If your answer is true, you can have anything you wish," King Arthur promised.

"Women want sovereignty over themselves. They want to make their own decisions," Ragnell snorted. "And my price is marriage to a knight of your court!"

King Arthur was sickened by this trick. To marry one of his men to this hideous thing! But he was caught in his promise.

"I'll marry you," said Gawain. "If King Arthur lives, you will be my bride."

King Arthur returned to the witch with Ragnell's answer. He lived. Gawain, true to his word, married the foul Ragnell. The wedding party watched with horror as all through the wedding feast the bride belched, scratched, drooled, and cackled. She told raunchy stories that would make a sailor blush. Everyone pitied poor Gawain.

Poor, gallant Gawain climbed the steps to his wedding chamber to his unfortunate marriage. He shuddered at the thought of touching, much less coupling, with this monstrous woman. And there she was, leering at him as he entered the room. "Embrace me, husband!"

When Gawain took the hag in his arms, he discovered he was holding the most beautiful maiden he had ever seen! Her hair was silky and her complexion fair. Her body was lithe, and her eyes sparkled at him with adoration.

"Who are you?" Gawain asked as he glanced around the room for his wife.

"I am your wife," she smiled. "I was cursed to be as you knew me until I could win a true knight in marriage. You can have me as I am either by night or by day, but I must return to my hag form at those other times. Do you prefer me like this at night when I'm in your arms? Or do prefer me beautiful by day when I will be seen by your friends?"

Gawain thought for a long time. At last, he replied, "This must be your choice. You decide."

And in that moment, the spell was broken. Her return to choice freed her from the curse and returned her to her natural beauty.

The moral of this story? Bring love to what you find ugly and scary.

Choice is magical.

You will be challenged by things that look ugly in this life. That area of your greatest pain may be the key to what you want most.

This is alchemy: The transformation of leaden, human experience into spiritual gold.

EVOLUTION ACCELERATOR

Your new year can start now, the moment you open this journal. This is a great opportunity to examine what is ready to fall away in your life and what wants to be born in its place.

If you could make just one change in your life, what would it be?

What is in the way of what you want?

Are you ready to give up what is in the way?

Now's the time, Baby.

If you answered yes, you are ready for the next step:

Physicalize your intention.

In fact, this chapter is going to engage your senses, get you out of your head, and into your body, your intuition, and your whole self. If you want to make something happen, the more of yourself you use, the faster you'll see the results. And most of all, it's fun! Fun is the best way to get things done.

Evolution Accelerator

Write it down, this lesson that you are ready to release. Then, preferably at some night that is important to you, (Full Moon, New Moon, tonight), burn it and send it on its way. (For instance, you may have learned the lesson of chronic illness, or low self-esteem, or bad relationships, or poverty, or lack of auditions—you're ready to move on!) Next, request a lesson you want in its place, so as not to leave a vacuum. (You may want to request the lesson of full vitality, self-love, prosperity, or full employment in its place, so that you can take the lessons you've already learned and go out and fully realize your potential in the world.)

Then, and this is the **most important part of the ritual**, drink some good champagne or eat some fantastic chocolate cake, juicy fruit, or something truly delicious, and affirm in your heart that you are accepting the new lesson with every sip and bite. Accept it into your body, your very cells, and have a party!

Special Bonus: Scan this QR code on your smartphone for my special video to guide you through the Evolution Accelerator process.

You can also access it here: https://www.morganarae.com/9LJ3h

CREATE A THEME

Take a deep breath. Feel your heart open.

See yourself twelve months from now, looking back on the best year of your life. You feel great about yourself! You have accomplished every goal you set.

> **Where do you live a year from now?**
> **Who is in your life?**
> **What do you do for work?**
> **What do you for fun?**
> **What was the defining quality that carried you forward?**
> **What was the *theme* of your year?**

Your theme *sets your direction* and keeps you on course in the face of unpredictable events. Opportunities arise mysteriously. Your theme will carry you forward. Your theme will help you know how to respond.

A theme is bigger than your individual goals. (It's not a new car, a television series, or getting over that rat who broke your heart.) Your theme creates a *context* for your goals. Some of the best themes I've seen at work include, "play a bigger game," "gracious receiver," "fun," "partnership," "expansion," "love," "appreciation," "unstoppable."

Your theme will be the filter for your whole life over the next twelve months.

For instance, if your theme was "play a bigger game," how might you play a bigger game at home, at work, in your relationships, in health? Or what might be possible if everything was about "partnership?" Get the picture?

What theme would best serve your happiness and success for the next twelve months?

Listen for resonance. The answer may surprise you.

CREATE YOUR YEAR

Now that you have chosen your theme, what would be possible at the end of twelve months… living your theme? What *wants to happen* in your life?

Use your intuition. Listen with your inner ear. Look with your inner eye. No matter how information comes to you, let it come to you now.

These are your goals!

Look at your goals for the next twelve months. Block out the goals you'd like to start in the first quarter of the year, second, third or fourth. **You don't have to do everything at once!** Some of your goals you may choose to focus on for several quarters, even the whole year, like self-care or networking. Other goals may be more time specific, like sell a script, take a vacation, buy a house, build a website. See if you can focus on only two or three goals each quarter.

What will *your* year look like?

Goal	1st Qtr.	2nd Qtr.	3rd Qtr.	4th Qtr.

THE MANIFESTATION SYSTEM

Every three months, fill out the <u>Quarterly Intention Form</u>:

1) Use the Life Wheel each quarter to grade every area of life satisfaction from zero, (couldn't be worse), to ten, (totally rocks). **What would make each area closer to a ten?** Use your notes from the end of the book to get clearer about this.

2) Remind yourself of this year's theme.

3) Read this quarter's Magic Accelerator. This is your focus for the next three months.

4) Pick three professional and three personal goals for the next three months. *These goals may include goals from the "Create Your Year" grid, or you can plug in other goals that are important to you now.*

5) Eliminate things in your life that no longer serve you.

6) Make a wish. This is where you *co-create* something wonderful with the universe. Make your wish realistic… but it's something that could use a little divine intervention too.

7) For life balance, find one small action to improve your score in each area of your wheel of life.

Every Sunday night, set your intentions in the <u>Weekly Journal</u>:

1) Set your top priorities. What actions are most important this week?

2) Anything else (for Life Balance) is *extra* credit for the karma bank. You can leave spaces blank.

3) Keep talking to Money! Each week ask what you could do to make Money happy to be with you. What loving action can you take to make your relationship with Money better?

4) The Chinese character for "Challenge" is the same as "Opportunity." What are your challenges this week? What opportunities do they present?

5) What can you ask for from the universe this week? Maybe it's a short line at the DMV, a good meeting, a new client, a hot date, a sales goal. Put it out there and see what shows up. Treat it like a game.

During the Week:

1) Record at least five successes each day before you go to sleep. Some successes may be big, some small. (Ever had a day when getting out of bed was a victory? Then count that as a success!) Human beings have success amnesia: We forget the positive things what we've done almost as soon as we've done it. Keep a record!

2) Find evidence of your prosperity every day. Prosperity shows up in many ways: money, health, relationships, talent, or fun. Acknowledge how rich your life is. Build your case. Thank you Money! Thank you Universe!

End the Week:

1) End the week with gratitude. How many things about yourself, your life, the planet, or existence itself can you appreciate? Tune into everything you love.

2) What did you learn this week? How will you use your insight?

End of the Quarter:

1) What were the highlights of the last three months? What did you learn? Celebrate your accomplishments, evaluate your progress, and set yourself up for even more success!

First Quarter

❖ ❖ ❖

"My new relationship with my money has changed everything for the better. I am so grateful, so relieved, so happy.

This is the most difficult time of my entire life (and I've had quite a life!!!). Leaving my husband, having two young kids to take care of, following the suggestions of my money through all of it. I have been led into absolutely uncharted land.

Through all of it, my Money has been true, loving, brilliant, miraculous and steady. This has translated into ME being all of those things. I get it. I am getting it more and more. I have fully handed over everything to my Money. He is in charge, and I follow his direction. No matter what.

My mortgage company called and asked us if we would like to refinance our house at a lower rate and they would cover all the expenses. Called us!!!!! Is that a miracle or what? It turns out that I will be able to refinance, they will also pay off a huge credit card debt and our payment will still be less per month.

That's just one huge example. That's a real world miracle. But for me, the REAL miracle is that I feel empowered, ready, of service to the world in a big way and excited for everything. I know I will be able to give my kids the life I desire for them. I know I will give myself an amazing life.

My Money has big plans for me and I'm totally game!

— Athena Burke, New York

❖ ❖ ❖

NOTES

First Quarter Intentions

Eliminate Tolerations

Stop settling! What energy and joy drainers are you ready to handle?

Workplace

Home & Personal

Make A Wish

What's the big thing you want to have happen this quarter?

This Year's Theme

_____

Magic Accelerator

Make Space for What I Want

Top Three Professional Goals

1.

2.

3.

Top Three Personal Goals

1.

2.

3.

Life Balance: What small step would improve each area of your Life Wheel?

Career _____   Money _____   Recreation _____

Environment _____   Personal Growth _____   Health _____

Friends _____   Family _____   Romance_____

LIFE SATISFACTION ASSESSMENT

On a scale of one (needs work) to ten (fabulous), how would you relate your level of satisfaction in each area of the wheel below?

If an area isn't a "ten," what would make it a ten?

Write your responses on the next page.

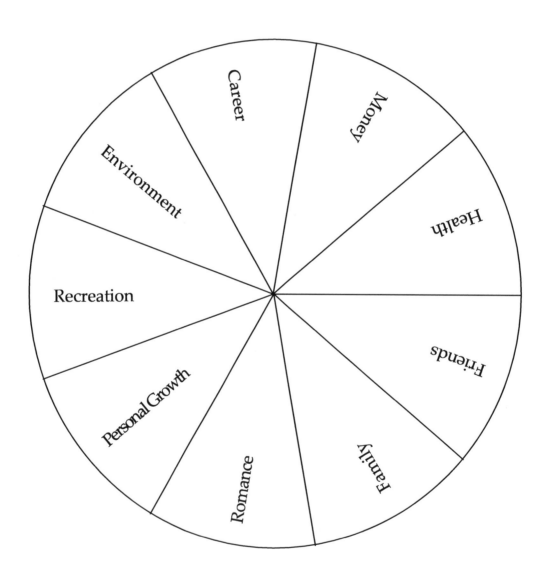

What's the gap between where you are and where you want to be?
What's the next step to move towards your ten?

Career

Money

Health

Friends

Family

Romance

Personal Growth

Recreation

Physical Environment

MAGIC ACCELERATOR

Make Space for What You Want

> *"I have never been more clear on how much I allowed that went against my grain...*
>
> *I love myself so much more than I ever have. I trust myself. I am completely stress-free. When I look in my eyes, I see beauty. When I think of myself, I feel ennobled. When I speak to myself, it is with the utmost respect. I am totally focused on my senses and pleasure.*
>
> *I have been paid in tough lessons that are truly priceless — now money can finally be attracted to me because I have become irresistable. I no longer chase money. It comes to me."*
>
> *— Shakaya Leone, Canada*
> *www.earthempress.com*

> *"It takes a lot of courage to release the familiar and seemingly secure, to embrace the new. But there is no real security in what is no longer meaningful. There is more security in the adventurous and exciting, for in movement there is life, and in change there is power."*
>
> *— Alan Cohen*

Would you like to create fast change? Here's how: Make room for what you want!

When clients are stuck and not manifesting their desired results, I have them take a look at what they're tolerating in their lives. What do they put up with that drains their energy? Where are they settling?

We all have tolerations: those people, things, or habits that drain our energy, dim our life enjoyment. It could be a messy desk, a critical relative, or not taking care of your health. We may have become so accustomed to certain tolerations that we feel that's just the way life is. We don't think we have a choice. We feel powerless, and that sense of powerlessness bleeds into other areas of our lives.

Every time you settle, you are telling the universe that "This is good enough," and you are telling yourself, "I don't deserve better." If that's your message, of course you'll keep getting more of the same! When your life is full of settling, you aren't leaving room for what you really want.

To help you identify where you may be settling, review the Life Wheel you just filled out three pages ago. Pick the wedges that represent areas of your life you find the least satisfying. What could you eliminate from each wedge to make more room?

Paying attention to what you are ready to eliminate is key. Maybe you're ready for a big change. Don't beat yourself up if you're not. I recommend starting small as a little change goes a long way. The smallest changes build your energy and confidence and give you a platform for the next change.

Try giving old clothes away to charity, clearing your desk, or spending less time with a critical friend. When you clear something up in one area of your life, you've created energetic space that will impact the rest of your life. My clients have won awards, received money out of the blue, attracted new business, and found soulmates after they stopped settling in other areas of their lives. When in doubt, clean your house.

I've come to believe that creating space is one of the fastest keys to attraction. Saying no to what no longer serves you will build your confidence and energy.

Sometimes when you make a big change, the universe will test you by sending you more of the same, (same type of client, same type of job, same type of relationship), to see if you're serious. Keep asking yourself what you want and who you want to be, and is this a good fit for who you're becoming?

Hold out for what you really want. Review your Wish List. Add to it. Use your list to help you recognize your wishes when they appear.

Weekly Journal

From _____ to _____.

Top Priorities

These actions are my top priorities this week. Anything else is for fairy points.

☐ _____

☐ _____

☐ _____

☐ _____

☐ _____

Make Money Happy

_____

Magic Strategy: Make Space

Eliminate the tolerations.

Challenges

Opportunities

Request Assistance from The Universe

What I would like help with this week.

_____

Life Balance: *You get fairy points for just one small action in each area:*

Career_____ Money_____ Recreation _____

Environment _____ Pers. Growth _____ Health_____

Friends _____ Family_____ Romance_____

Success Journal

Monday
1
2
3
4
5
Tuesday
1
2
3
4
5
Wednesday
1
2
3
4
5
Thursday
1
2
3
4
5
Friday
1
2
3
4
5
Saturday
1
2
3
4
5
Sunday
1
2
3
4
5

Make Money Happy Daily

Monday

Tuesday

Wednesday

Thursday

Friday

Saturday

Sunday

Gratitude

What I am grateful for this week:

Learning

What I learned about myself this week:

 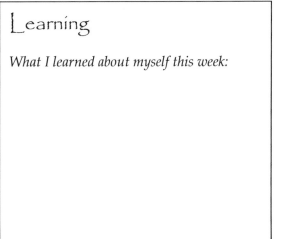

Weekly Journal

From _____ to _____.

Top Priorities

*These actions are my top priorities this week.
Anything else is for fairy points.*

☐ _____

☐ _____

☐ _____

☐ _____

☐ _____

Make Money Happy

_____

Magic Strategy:
Make Space

Eliminate the tolerations.

Challenges

Opportunities

Request Assistance from The Universe

What I would like help with this week.

_____

Life Balance: *You get fairy points for just one small action in each area:*

Career_____ Money_____ Recreation _____

Environment _____ Pers. Growth _____ Health_____

Friends _____ Family_____ Romance_____

Success Journal

Monday
1
2
3
4
5
Tuesday
1
2
3
4
5
Wednesday
1
2
3
4
5
Thursday
1
2
3
4
5
Friday
1
2
3
4
5
Saturday
1
2
3
4
5
Sunday
1
2
3
4
5

Make Money Happy Daily

Monday

Tuesday

Wednesday

Thursday

Friday

Saturday

Sunday

Gratitude

What I am grateful for this week:

Learning

What I learned about myself this week:

Weekly Journal

From _____ to _____.

Top Priorities

These actions are my top priorities this week. Anything else is for fairy points.

☐ _____

☐ _____

☐ _____

☐ _____

☐ _____

Make Money Happy

_____

Magic Strategy: Make Space

Eliminate the tolerations.

Challenges

Opportunities

Request Assistance from The Universe

What I would like help with this week.

_____

Life Balance: *You get fairy points for just one small action in each area:*

Career_____ Money_____ Recreation _____

Environment _____ Pers. Growth _____ Health_____

Friends _____ Family_____ Romance_____

Success Journal

Monday
1
2
3
4
5
Tuesday
1
2
3
4
5
Wednesday
1
2
3
4
5
Thursday
1
2
3
4
5
Friday
1
2
3
4
5
Saturday
1
2
3
4
5
Sunday
1
2
3
4
5

Make Money Happy Daily

Monday

Tuesday

Wednesday

Thursday

Friday

Saturday

Sunday

Gratitude

What I am grateful for this week:

Learning

What I learned about myself this week:

Weekly Journal

From _____ to _____.

Top Priorities

These actions are my top priorities this week. Anything else is for fairy points.

☐ _____

☐ _____

☐ _____

☐ _____

☐ _____

Make Money Happy

_____

Magic Strategy: Make Space

Eliminate the tolerations.

Challenges

Opportunities

Request Assistance from The Universe

What I would like help with this week.

_____

Life Balance: *You get fairy points for just one small action in each area:*

Career_____ Money_____ Recreation _____

Environment _____ Pers. Growth _____ Health_____

Friends _____ Family_____ Romance_____

Success Journal

Monday
1
2
3
4
5
Tuesday
1
2
3
4
5
Wednesday
1
2
3
4
5
Thursday
1
2
3
4
5
Friday
1
2
3
4
5
Saturday
1
2
3
4
5
Sunday
1
2
3
4
5

Make Money Happy Daily

Monday

Tuesday

Wednesday

Thursday

Friday

Saturday

Sunday

Gratitude

What I am grateful for this week:

Learning

What I learned about myself this week:

Weekly Journal

From _____ to _____.

Top Priorities

These actions are my top priorities this week. Anything else is for fairy points.

☐ _____

☐ _____

☐ _____

☐ _____

☐ _____

Make Money Happy

_____

Magic Strategy: Make Space

Eliminate the tolerations.

Challenges

Opportunities

Request Assistance from The Universe

What I would like help with this week.

_____

Life Balance: *You get fairy points for just one small action in each area:*

Career_____ Money_____ Recreation _____

Environment _____ Pers. Growth _____ Health_____

Friends _____ Family_____ Romance_____

Success Journal

Monday
1
2
3
4
5
Tuesday
1
2
3
4
5
Wednesday
1
2
3
4
5
Thursday
1
2
3
4
5
Friday
1
2
3
4
5
Saturday
1
2
3
4
5
Sunday
1
2
3
4
5

Make Money Happy Daily

Monday

Tuesday

Wednesday

Thursday

Friday

Saturday

Sunday

Gratitude

What I am grateful for this week:

Learning

What I learned about myself this week:

Weekly Journal

From _____ to _____.

Top Priorities

These actions are my top priorities this week.
Anything else is for fairy points.

☐ _____

☐ _____

☐ _____

☐ _____

☐ _____

Make Money Happy

_____

Magic Strategy: Make Space

Eliminate the tolerations.

Challenges

Opportunities

Request Assistance from The Universe

What I would like help with this week.

_____

Life Balance: *You get fairy points for just one small action in each area:*

Career_____ Money_____ Recreation _____

Environment _____ Pers. Growth _____ Health_____

Friends _____ Family_____ Romance_____

Success Journal

Monday
1
2
3
4
5
Tuesday
1
2
3
4
5
Wednesday
1
2
3
4
5
Thursday
1
2
3
4
5
Friday
1
2
3
4
5
Saturday
1
2
3
4
5
Sunday
1
2
3
4
5

Make Money Happy Daily

Monday

Tuesday

Wednesday

Thursday

Friday

Saturday

Sunday

Gratitude

What I am grateful for this week:

Learning

What I learned about myself this week:

Weekly Journal

From _____ to _____.

Top Priorities

These actions are my top priorities this week. Anything else is for fairy points.

☐ _____

☐ _____

☐ _____

☐ _____

☐ _____

Make Money Happy

_____

Magic Strategy: Make Space

Eliminate the tolerations.

Challenges

Opportunities

Request Assistance from The Universe

What I would like help with this week.

_____

Life Balance: *You get fairy points for just one small action in each area:*

Career_____ Money_____ Recreation _____

Environment _____ Pers. Growth _____ Health_____

Friends _____ Family_____ Romance_____

Success Journal

Monday
1
2
3
4
5
Tuesday
1
2
3
4
5
Wednesday
1
2
3
4
5
Thursday
1
2
3
4
5
Friday
1
2
3
4
5
Saturday
1
2
3
4
5
Sunday
1
2
3
4
5

Make Money Happy Daily

Monday

Tuesday

Wednesday

Thursday

Friday

Saturday

Sunday

Gratitude

What I am grateful for this week:

Learning

What I learned about myself this week:

Weekly Journal

From _____ to _____.

Top Priorities

These actions are my top priorities this week. Anything else is for fairy points.

☐ _____

☐ _____

☐ _____

☐ _____

☐ _____

Magic Strategy: Make Space

Eliminate the tolerations.

Challenges

Opportunities

Make Money Happy

_____

Request Assistance from The Universe

What I would like help with this week.

_____

Life Balance: *You get fairy points for just one small action in each area:*

Career_____ Money_____ Recreation _____

Environment _____ Pers. Growth _____ Health_____

Friends _____ Family_____ Romance_____

Success Journal

Monday
1
2
3
4
5
Tuesday
1
2
3
4
5
Wednesday
1
2
3
4
5
Thursday
1
2
3
4
5
Friday
1
2
3
4
5
Saturday
1
2
3
4
5
Sunday
1
2
3
4
5

Make Money Happy Daily

Monday

Tuesday

Wednesday

Thursday

Friday

Saturday

Sunday

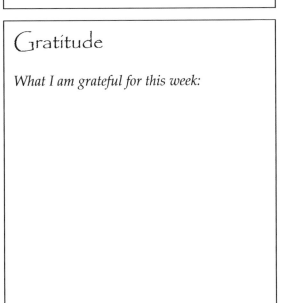

Gratitude

What I am grateful for this week:

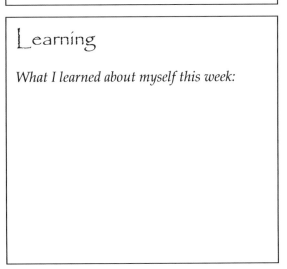

Learning

What I learned about myself this week:

Weekly Journal

From _____ to _____.

Top Priorities

*These actions are my top priorities this week.
Anything else is for fairy points.*

☐ _____

☐ _____

☐ _____

☐ _____

☐ _____

Make Money Happy

_____

Magic Strategy:
Make Space

Eliminate the tolerations.

Challenges

Opportunities

Request Assistance from The Universe

What I would like help with this week.

_____

Life Balance: *You get fairy points for just one small action in each area:*

Career _____ Money _____ Recreation _____

Environment _____ Pers. Growth _____ Health _____

Friends _____ Family _____ Romance _____

Success Journal

Monday
1
2
3
4
5
Tuesday
1
2
3
4
5
Wednesday
1
2
3
4
5
Thursday
1
2
3
4
5
Friday
1
2
3
4
5
Saturday
1
2
3
4
5
Sunday
1
2
3
4
5

Make Money Happy Daily

Monday

Tuesday

Wednesday

Thursday

Friday

Saturday

Sunday

Gratitude

What I am grateful for this week:

Learning

What I learned about myself this week:

Weekly Journal

From _____ to _____.

Top Priorities

These actions are my top priorities this week. Anything else is for fairy points.

☐ _____

☐ _____

☐ _____

☐ _____

☐ _____

Make Money Happy

_____

Magic Strategy: Make Space

Eliminate the tolerations.

Challenges

Opportunities

Request Assistance from The Universe

What I would like help with this week.

_____

Life Balance: *You get fairy points for just one small action in each area:*

Career_____ Money_____ Recreation _____

Environment _____ Pers. Growth _____ Health_____

Friends _____ Family_____ Romance_____

Success Journal

Monday
1
2
3
4
5
Tuesday
1
2
3
4
5
Wednesday
1
2
3
4
5
Thursday
1
2
3
4
5
Friday
1
2
3
4
5
Saturday
1
2
3
4
5
Sunday
1
2
3
4
5

Make Money Happy Daily

Monday

Tuesday

Wednesday

Thursday

Friday

Saturday

Sunday

Gratitude

What I am grateful for this week:

Learning

What I learned about myself this week:

Weekly Journal

From _____ to _____.

Top Priorities

These actions are my top priorities this week. Anything else is for fairy points.

☐ _____

☐ _____

☐ _____

☐ _____

☐ _____

Make Money Happy

_____

Magic Strategy: Make Space

Eliminate the tolerations.

Challenges

Opportunities

Request Assistance from The Universe

What I would like help with this week.

_____

Life Balance: *You get fairy points for just one small action in each area:*

Career_____ Money_____ Recreation _____

Environment _____ Pers. Growth _____ Health_____

Friends _____ Family_____ Romance_____

Success Journal

Monday
1
2
3
4
5
Tuesday
1
2
3
4
5
Wednesday
1
2
3
4
5
Thursday
1
2
3
4
5
Friday
1
2
3
4
5
Saturday
1
2
3
4
5
Sunday
1
2
3
4
5

Make Money Happy Daily

Monday

Tuesday

Wednesday

Thursday

Friday

Saturday

Sunday

Gratitude

What I am grateful for this week:

Learning

What I learned about myself this week:

Weekly Journal

From _____ to _____.

Top Priorities

These actions are my top priorities this week.
Anything else is for fairy points.

☐ _____

☐ _____

☐ _____

☐ _____

☐ _____

Make Money Happy

_____

Magic Strategy: Make Space

Eliminate the tolerations.

Challenges

Opportunities

Request Assistance from The Universe

What I would like help with this week.

_____

Life Balance: *You get fairy points for just one small action in each area:*

Career_____ Money_____ Recreation _____

Environment _____ Pers. Growth _____ Health_____

Friends _____ Family_____ Romance_____

Success Journal

Monday
1
2
3
4
5
Tuesday
1
2
3
4
5
Wednesday
1
2
3
4
5
Thursday
1
2
3
4
5
Friday
1
2
3
4
5
Saturday
1
2
3
4
5
Sunday
1
2
3
4
5

Make Money Happy Daily

Monday

Tuesday

Wednesday

Thursday

Friday

Saturday

Sunday

Gratitude

What I am grateful for this week:

Learning

What I learned about myself this week:

Weekly Journal

From _____ to _____.

Top Priorities

These actions are my top priorities this week. Anything else is for fairy points.

☐ _____

☐ _____

☐ _____

☐ _____

☐ _____

Make Money Happy

_____

Magic Strategy: Make Space

Eliminate the tolerations.

Challenges

Opportunities

Request Assistance from The Universe

What I would like help with this week.

_____

Life Balance: *You get fairy points for just one small action in each area:*

Career_____ Money_____ Recreation _____

Environment _____ Pers. Growth _____ Health_____

Friends _____ Family_____ Romance_____

Success Journal

Monday
1
2
3
4
5
Tuesday
1
2
3
4
5
Wednesday
1
2
3
4
5
Thursday
1
2
3
4
5
Friday
1
2
3
4
5
Saturday
1
2
3
4
5
Sunday
1
2
3
4
5

Make Money Happy Daily

Monday

Tuesday

Wednesday

Thursday

Friday

Saturday

Sunday

Gratitude

What I am grateful for this week:

Learning

What I learned about myself this week:

FIRST QUARTER HIGHLIGHTS
AND LEARNINGS

Accomplishments	What I Learned	Next Step

What did I do really well this quarter?

In what area of my life did I grow the most?

What is the most important thing I learned about myself?

How can I give myself even better results in the future?

Second Quarter

❖ ❖ ❖

"When I first heard about creating a romantic relationship with money, I was a bit uncomfortable with the idea of having a romantic relationship with another "man," even if he was only imaginary, because I love my husband very much. However, instead of compromising my relationship with my husband, I discovered that having my Money Honey loving me completely and supporting me fully helped my marriage immensely!

Suddenly because I was being supported perfectly in all the ways I needed support; I was able to love my husband so much more. I was amazed, and my husband immediately noticed the difference.

With the love and support of my Money Honey in place, I was able to allow my husband to just be himself, imperfections and all. My husband was no longer responsible for filling all the needsI had that he just couldn't fill (as wonderful as he is) and that really aren't his job to fill to begin with and are unfair for me to expect him to fill anyway! Now my Money Honey is there to fill that void.

I'm completely astounded by all the areas of my life that have changed by changing my relationship with money."

– Kirsten Nelson, Boise, Idaho

❖ ❖ ❖

NOTES

Second Quarter Intentions

Eliminate Tolerations

Stop settling! What energy and joy drainers are you ready to handle?

Workplace

Home & Personal

Make A Wish

What's the big thing you want to have happen this quarter?

This Year's Theme

_____

Magic Accelerator

Networking Magic

Top Three Professional Goals

1.

2.

3.

Top Three Personal Goals

1.

2.

3.

Life Balance: What small step would improve each area of your Life Wheel?

Career _____ Money _____ Recreation _____

Environment _____ Personal Growth _____ Health _____

Friends _____ Family _____ Romance _____

LIFE SATISFACTION ASSESSMENT

On a scale of one (needs work) to ten (fabulous), how would you relate your level of satisfaction in each area of the wheel below?

If an area isn't a "ten," what would make it a ten?

Write your responses on the next page.

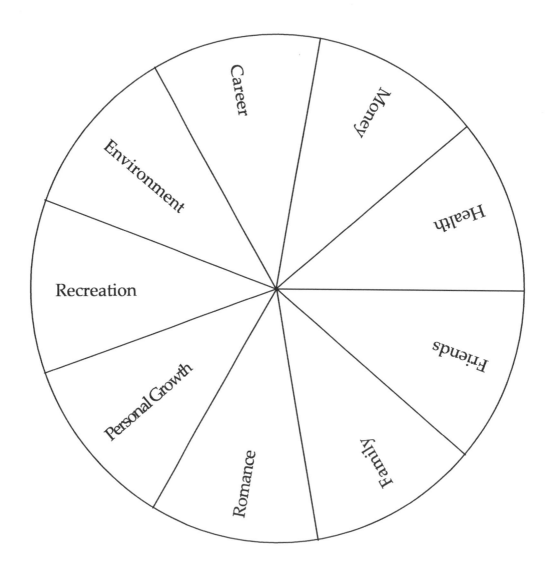

What's the gap between where you are and where you want to be?
What's the next step to move towards your ten?

Career

Money

Health

Friends

Family

Romance

Personal Growth

Recreation

Physical Environment

MAGIC ACCELERATOR

Networking Magic

"I honor your Gods.
I drink from your well.
I bring an unprotected heart to our meeting place.
I hold no cherished outcome.
I will not negotiate by withholding. I am not subject to disappointment."

— Druid vow of friendship

Let this vow be your guide to networking. Meet. Respect. Connect. Release attachment to results.

Networking is not selling. Think of what it's like when a stranger comes up and sells at you and shoves you his business card. This is a relationship killer, even at a "networking" party!

Be the person who builds relationships.

There's a principle in relationship that you should take to heart: If one party is chasing, the other is retreating. You don't want to be the chaser. Attraction is far more magical. Everything I share in this article will be with an eye towards accelerating your powers of attraction.

As you set out on your networking journey, hoping to attract lots of business, ask yourself what *your* dream customers want.

- Are you really selling what your people want?
- Or are you trying to get people to buy what you're selling?

"I have no trouble believing this, but it's such a gas!!!!! 2 days after working with your e-book, my husband received a

$5,500 unexpected bonus! I just received your workbook, and began working with it last night.

Well, today my husband received a

$550 increase a month AFTER

taxes, income. This allows us to buy the new car, and model, I really want! (My car, which I still love, is 12 years old—so it certainly is time!). WOW!

I am a self employed singer, songwriter, musician, children's teaching artist.

My field is feeling the recession, friends in the field are really worried, phones are not ringing, budgets are cut back... BUT MY BUSINESS IS BOOMING.

$3800 worth of booking has come in within the past 2 days.

And I know it's just the beginning of money magic this year. I feel joyful and free! THANK YOU MORGANA!

THANK YOU MONEY HONEY!!!"

-Anna

You'll find most people want improvement in the same areas: money, love, career, health, and happiness. By connecting and creating relationships, you will have the opportunity to discover what your ideal customers want, and to examine how you might serve their needs.

With this knowledge as your foundation, you can create networking magic: Customers who seek you out and spread the word. (And the people who are not meant to be your customers may still become your dearest friends and fans.)

Five Secrets to Networking Magic

1) Be authentic! Can you think of a time when you felt centered in who you are, comfortable in your own skin? You had a strong connection to your inherent value, and you weren't worried about the judgments of others. This is the foundation of everything. You can't build a relationship if you're not really there.

   There are really two kinds of people: your people and not your people. It's easy to tell the difference. *Your* people get you and appreciate you. The others don't. I believe it's a waste of time and heart to try to convince those who aren't your people to become your people. Let them go. If you excel at authenticity, you will repel the people who are not right for you so that your people can find you!

   This can be scary. It's also very attractive.

2) Do what you enjoy! If you don't like to do something, dump or delegate it. Growing your network takes persistence, a steady flow of new relationships. You are so much more likely to keep going and see good results if you pick activities that you naturally like. What is the easiest, most pleasurable way for you to connect with people?

   I enjoy writing, so I stay in contact with thousands of people every month through email and my newsletter. My best friend fills her practice by meeting people over coffee. I know a coach who loves to talk on the phone, so cold calls are like candy to her.

   And how about parties? You can meet the most fantastic new people at your own parties. (When I was an in the entertainment industry, I would meet producers, directors, and movie stars at my own parties. I became known for introducing people who could work together.)

   Do what is the most fun for you. Imagine letting go of your "should" networking activities, anything that feels like heavy lifting, and focusing on ways to connect that are fun for you. How much more energy would you have if you refused to do anything but play?

3) Focus on the other person! Seek first how you can help others, not how they can hire you. It's really not about you. Tune in to their concerns. Connect the people you meet to *other* people and resources that could help them. Be the 'go-to' person. Trust that you will get your share.

   People buy from sources they like and trust. You must create that connection first. The more you give freely from your heart, the more you build the trust and relationship that will move you forward personally and professionally.

4) Plant and release! Plant a LOT and release… and do it again. Without attachment. Not every seed bears fruit. Your job is to keep planting. Keep meeting and helping, and above all, doing what you love. A tree can't grow if you keep digging up the roots. Allow the invisible to happen before you see the fruit. And let the fruit surprise you.

5) Be willing to be visible! Just because you are not attracting strangers with sales pitches does not mean you are to hide who you are and what you do. Practice showing up. Be ready when people ask, "What do you do?"

   And if people are interested, let them taste. Give them a nice appetizer, not the whole five course dinner. Set the necessary boundaries to take care of yourself but have the confidence that you can afford to share. This can include giving samples, writing articles, posting on forums, volunteering for a cause, or just sharing your expertise. Think outside the box for more ideas. You are not pushing anything, but you are raising your visibility and creating opportunities for your people to discover your value.

One last word on networking magic comes from the ancient Indian legend of Indra's Net. According to myth, this net stretches out across the universe, with a multifaceted jewel sitting at every intersection. Each facet of each jewel reflects every other jewel in the system. Everything is connected and reflects everything else. This is our condition as human beings. We are those jewels, connected and designed to reflect the brilliant gem essence in everyone else.

Work Indra's Net! See every person you meet as a jewel that holds the universe together. There is no separation, just reflection. What does that make possible? Your network is limitless.

Weekly Journal

From _____ to _____.

Top Priorities

These actions are my top priorities this week. Anything else is for fairy points.

☐ _____

☐ _____

☐ _____

☐ _____

☐ _____

Make Money Happy

_____

Magic Strategy:

Network Magic

How can I help others get what they want?

Challenges

Opportunities

Request Assistance from The Universe

What I would like help with this week.

_____

Life Balance: What small step would improve each of these areas of your life?

Career_____ Money_____ Recreation_____

Environment_____ Personal Growth_____ Health_____

Friends_____ Family_____ Romance_____

Success Journal

Monday
1
2
3
4
5
Tuesday
1
2
3
4
5
Wednesday
1
2
3
4
5
Thursday
1
2
3
4
5
Friday
1
2
3
4
5
Saturday
1
2
3
4
5
Sunday
1
2
3
4
5

Make Money Happy Daily

Monday

Tuesday

Wednesday

Thursday

Friday

Saturday

Sunday

Gratitude

What I am grateful for this week:

Learning

What I learned about myself this week:

Weekly Journal

From _____ to _____.

Top Priorities

These actions are my top priorities this week. Anything else is for fairy points.

☐ _____

☐ _____

☐ _____

☐ _____

☐ _____

Make Money Happy

_____

Magic Strategy:

Network Magic

How can I help others get what they want?

Challenges

Opportunities

Request Assistance from The Universe

What I would like help with this week.

_____

Life Balance: What small step would improve each of these areas of your life?

Career_____ Money_____ Recreation_____

Environment_____ Personal Growth_____ Health_____

Friends_____ Family_____ Romance_____

Success Journal

Monday
1
2
3
4
5
Tuesday
1
2
3
4
5
Wednesday
1
2
3
4
5
Thursday
1
2
3
4
5
Friday
1
2
3
4
5
Saturday
1
2
3
4
5
Sunday
1
2
3
4
5

Make Money Happy Daily

Monday

Tuesday

Wednesday

Thursday

Friday

Saturday

Sunday

Gratitude

What I am grateful for this week:

Learning

What I learned about myself this week:

Weekly Journal

From _____ to _____.

Top Priorities

These actions are my top priorities this week. Anything else is for fairy points.

☐ _____

☐ _____

☐ _____

☐ _____

☐ _____

Make Money Happy

_____

Magic Strategy:

Network Magic

How can I help others get what they want?

Challenges

Opportunities

Request Assistance from The Universe

What I would like help with this week.

_____

Life Balance: What small step would improve each of these areas of your life?

Career_____   Money_____   Recreation_____

Environment_____   Personal Growth_____   Health_____

Friends_____   Family_____   Romance_____

Success Journal

Monday
1
2
3
4
5
Tuesday
1
2
3
4
5
Wednesday
1
2
3
4
5
Thursday
1
2
3
4
5
Friday
1
2
3
4
5
Saturday
1
2
3
4
5
Sunday
1
2
3
4
5

Make Money Happy Daily

Monday

Tuesday

Wednesday

Thursday

Friday

Saturday

Sunday

Gratitude

What I am grateful for this week:

Learning

What I learned about myself this week:

Weekly Journal

From _____ to _____.

Top Priorities

These actions are my top priorities this week. Anything else is for fairy points.

☐ _____

☐ _____

☐ _____

☐ _____

☐ _____

Make Money Happy

_____

Magic Strategy:

Network Magic

How can I help others get what they want?

Challenges

Opportunities

Request Assistance from The Universe

What I would like help with this week.

_____

Life Balance: What small step would improve each of these areas of your life?

Career_____   Money_____   Recreation_____

Environment_____   Personal Growth_____   Health_____

Friends_____   Family_____   Romance_____

Success Journal

Monday
1
2
3
4
5
Tuesday
1
2
3
4
5
Wednesday
1
2
3
4
5
Thursday
1
2
3
4
5
Friday
1
2
3
4
5
Saturday
1
2
3
4
5
Sunday
1
2
3
4
5

Make Money Happy Daily

Monday

Tuesday

Wednesday

Thursday

Friday

Saturday

Sunday

Gratitude

What I am grateful for this week:

Learning

What I learned about myself this week:

 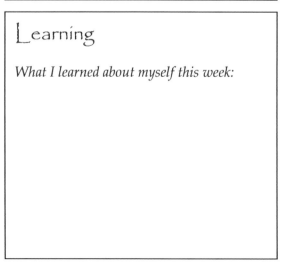

Weekly Journal

From _____ to _____.

Top Priorities

These actions are my top priorities this week.
Anything else is for fairy points.

☐ _____

☐ _____

☐ _____

☐ _____

☐ _____

Make Money Happy

_____

Magic Strategy:

Network Magic

How can I help others get what they want?

Challenges

Opportunities

Request Assistance from The Universe

What I would like help with this week.

_____

Life Balance: What small step would improve each of these areas of your life?

Career_____   Money_____   Recreation_____

Environment_____   Personal Growth_____   Health_____

Friends_____   Family_____   Romance_____

Success Journal

Monday
1
2
3
4
5
Tuesday
1
2
3
4
5
Wednesday
1
2
3
4
5
Thursday
1
2
3
4
5
Friday
1
2
3
4
5
Saturday
1
2
3
4
5
Sunday
1
2
3
4
5

Make Money Happy Daily

Monday

Tuesday

Wednesday

Thursday

Friday

Saturday

Sunday

Gratitude

What I am grateful for this week:

Learning

What I learned about myself this week:

Weekly Journal

From _____ to _____.

Top Priorities

These actions are my top priorities this week.
Anything else is for fairy points.

☐ _____

☐ _____

☐ _____

☐ _____

☐ _____

Make Money Happy

_____

Magic Strategy:

Network Magic
How can I help others get what they want?

Challenges

Opportunities

Request Assistance from The Universe

What I would like help with this week.

_____

Life Balance: What small step would improve each of these areas of your life?

Career_____ Money_____ Recreation_____

Environment_____ Personal Growth_____ Health_____

Friends_____ Family_____ Romance_____

Success Journal

Monday
1
2
3
4
5
Tuesday
1
2
3
4
5
Wednesday
1
2
3
4
5
Thursday
1
2
3
4
5
Friday
1
2
3
4
5
Saturday
1
2
3
4
5
Sunday
1
2
3
4
5

Make Money Happy Daily

Monday

Tuesday

Wednesday

Thursday

Friday

Saturday

Sunday

Gratitude

What I am grateful for this week:

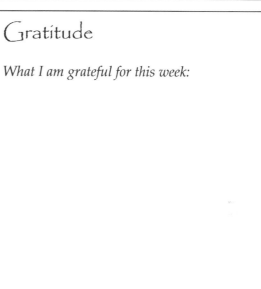

Learning

What I learned about myself this week:

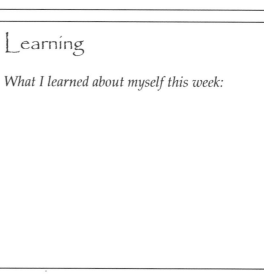

Weekly Journal

From _____ to _____.

Top Priorities

*These actions are my top priorities this week.
Anything else is for fairy points.*

☐ _____

☐ _____

☐ _____

☐ _____

☐ _____

Make Money Happy

_____

Magic Strategy:

Network Magic
*How can I help others get what they
want?*

Challenges

Opportunities

Request Assistance
from The Universe
What I would like help with this week.

_____

Life Balance: What small step would improve each of these areas of your life?

Career_____ Money_____ Recreation_____

Environment_____ Personal Growth_____ Health_____

Friends_____ Family_____ Romance_____

Success Journal

Monday
1
2
3
4
5
Tuesday
1
2
3
4
5
Wednesday
1
2
3
4
5
Thursday
1
2
3
4
5
Friday
1
2
3
4
5
Saturday
1
2
3
4
5
Sunday
1
2
3
4
5

Make Money Happy Daily

Monday

Tuesday

Wednesday

Thursday

Friday

Saturday

Sunday

Gratitude

What I am grateful for this week:

Learning

What I learned about myself this week:

Weekly Journal

From _____ to _____.

Top Priorities

These actions are my top priorities this week. Anything else is for fairy points.

☐ _____

☐ _____

☐ _____

☐ _____

☐ _____

Make Money Happy

_____

Magic Strategy:

Network Magic

How can I help others get what they want?

Challenges

Opportunities

Request Assistance from The Universe

What I would like help with this week.

_____

Life Balance: What small step would improve each of these areas of your life?

Career_____ Money_____ Recreation_____

Environment_____ Personal Growth_____ Health_____

Friends_____ Family_____ Romance_____

Success Journal

Monday
1
2
3
4
5
Tuesday
1
2
3
4
5
Wednesday
1
2
3
4
5
Thursday
1
2
3
4
5
Friday
1
2
3
4
5
Saturday
1
2
3
4
5
Sunday
1
2
3
4
5

Make Money Happy Daily

Monday

Tuesday

Wednesday

Thursday

Friday

Saturday

Sunday

Gratitude

What I am grateful for this week:

Learning

What I learned about myself this week:

Weekly Journal

From _____ to _____.

Top Priorities

These actions are my top priorities this week. Anything else is for fairy points.

☐ _____

☐ _____

☐ _____

☐ _____

☐ _____

Make Money Happy

_____

Magic Strategy:

Network Magic

How can I help others get what they want?

Challenges

Opportunities

Request Assistance from The Universe

What I would like help with this week.

_____

Life Balance: What small step would improve each of these areas of your life?

Career_____ Money_____ Recreation_____

Environment_____ Personal Growth_____ Health_____

Friends_____ Family_____ Romance_____

Success Journal

Monday
1
2
3
4
5
Tuesday
1
2
3
4
5
Wednesday
1
2
3
4
5
Thursday
1
2
3
4
5
Friday
1
2
3
4
5
Saturday
1
2
3
4
5
Sunday
1
2
3
4
5

Make Money Happy Daily

Monday

Tuesday

Wednesday

Thursday

Friday

Saturday

Sunday

Gratitude

What I am grateful for this week:

Learning

What I learned about myself this week:

 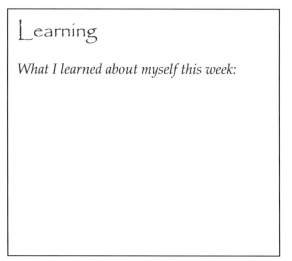

Weekly Journal

From _____ to _____.

Top Priorities

These actions are my top priorities this week. Anything else is for fairy points.

☐ _____

☐ _____

☐ _____

☐ _____

☐ _____

Make Money Happy

_____

Magic Strategy:

Network Magic

How can I help others get what they want?

Challenges

Opportunities

Request Assistance from The Universe

What I would like help with this week.

_____

Life Balance: What small step would improve each of these areas of your life?

Career_____ Money_____ Recreation_____

Environment_____ Personal Growth_____ Health_____

Friends_____ Family_____ Romance_____

Success Journal

Monday
1
2
3
4
5
Tuesday
1
2
3
4
5
Wednesday
1
2
3
4
5
Thursday
1
2
3
4
5
Friday
1
2
3
4
5
Saturday
1
2
3
4
5
Sunday
1
2
3
4
5

Make Money Happy Daily

Monday

Tuesday

Wednesday

Thursday

Friday

Saturday

Sunday

Gratitude

What I am grateful for this week:

Learning

What I learned about myself this week:

Weekly Journal

From _____ to _____.

Top Priorities

These actions are my top priorities this week. Anything else is for fairy points.

☐ _____

☐ _____

☐ _____

☐ _____

☐ _____

Make Money Happy

_____

Magic Strategy:

Network Magic

How can I help others get what they want?

Challenges

Opportunities

Request Assistance from The Universe

What I would like help with this week.

_____

Life Balance: What small step would improve each of these areas of your life?

Career_____ Money_____ Recreation_____

Environment_____ Personal Growth_____ Health_____

Friends_____ Family_____ Romance_____

Success Journal

Monday
1
2
3
4
5
Tuesday
1
2
3
4
5
Wednesday
1
2
3
4
5
Thursday
1
2
3
4
5
Friday
1
2
3
4
5
Saturday
1
2
3
4
5
Sunday
1
2
3
4
5

Make Money Happy Daily

Monday

Tuesday

Wednesday

Thursday

Friday

Saturday

Sunday

Gratitude

What I am grateful for this week:

Learning

What I learned about myself this week:

Weekly Journal

From _____ to _____.

Top Priorities

These actions are my top priorities this week. Anything else is for fairy points.

☐ _____

☐ _____

☐ _____

☐ _____

☐ _____

Make Money Happy

_____

Magic Strategy:

Network Magic

How can I help others get what they want?

Challenges

Opportunities

Request Assistance from The Universe

What I would like help with this week.

_____

Life Balance: What small step would improve each of these areas of your life?

Career_____   Money_____   Recreation_____

Environment_____   Personal Growth_____   Health_____

Friends_____   Family_____   Romance_____

Success Journal

Monday
1
2
3
4
5
Tuesday
1
2
3
4
5
Wednesday
1
2
3
4
5
Thursday
1
2
3
4
5
Friday
1
2
3
4
5
Saturday
1
2
3
4
5
Sunday
1
2
3
4
5

Make Money Happy Daily

Monday

Tuesday

Wednesday

Thursday

Friday

Saturday

Sunday

Gratitude

What I am grateful for this week:

Learning

What I learned about myself this week:

 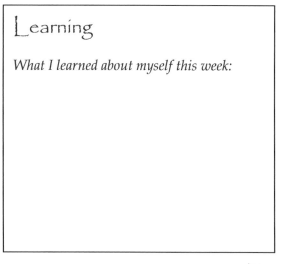

Weekly Journal

From _____ to _____.

Top Priorities

*These actions are my top priorities this week.
Anything else is for fairy points.*

☐ _____

☐ _____

☐ _____

☐ _____

☐ _____

Make Money Happy

_____

Magic Strategy:

Network Magic
*How can I help others get what they
want?*

Challenges

Opportunities

Request Assistance from The Universe
What I would like help with this week.

_____

Life Balance: What small step would improve each of these areas of your life?

Career_____   Money_____   Recreation_____

Environment_____   Personal Growth_____   Health_____

Friends_____   Family_____   Romance_____

Success Journal

Monday
1
2
3
4
5
Tuesday
1
2
3
4
5
Wednesday
1
2
3
4
5
Thursday
1
2
3
4
5
Friday
1
2
3
4
5
Saturday
1
2
3
4
5
Sunday
1
2
3
4
5

Make Money Happy Daily

Monday

Tuesday

Wednesday

Thursday

Friday

Saturday

Sunday

Gratitude

What I am grateful for this week:

Learning

What I learned about myself this week:

SECOND QUARTER HIGHLIGHTS
AND LEARNINGS

Accomplishments	What I Learned	Next Step

What did I do really well this quarter?

In what area of my life did I grow the most?

What is the most important thing I learned about myself?

How can I give myself even better results in the future?

Third Quarter

"I just have to tell you this. I listened to the teleclass you did last night — I found out about it an hour before it was scheduled and felt moved to attend. Wow, wow, wow! haven't even done the Money Monster exercise yet, but for some reason I totally connected with the idea of the Money Honey and got mine right away, plus an action to take. I took that action last night (set some financial boundaries with my adult children) and this morning two things happened.

I went to pay for parking outside Starbucks, 50 cents for 20 minutes. When I pushed the button for the ticket, the ticket came out, and $1.75 in change dropped into the coin return area!

I got an email from my ex-husband saying he and his wife would like to pay my $4000 property tax bill (which I can't pay)...this is without ANY solicitation on my part. And they insist this be a gift, not a loan.

So, in less than 24 hours, my Money Honey has not only radically changed my feelings about money,but he has also brought me $4,001.25 :)

Bless you!!!!! For the first time in 58 years, I am excited and positive to see what is going to happen for me financially. It's huge, really huge."

— Chansonette Buck

NOTES

Third Quarter Intentions

Eliminate Tolerations

Stop settling! What energy and joy drainers are you ready to handle?

Workplace

Home & Personal

Make A Wish

What's the big thing you want to have happen this quarter?

This Year's Theme

_____

Magic Accelerator

Stronger Boundaries

Top Three Professional Goals

1.

2.

3.

Top Three Personal Goals

1.

2.

3.

Life Balance: What small step would improve each area of your Life Wheel?

Career _____   Money _____   Recreation _____

Environment _____   Personal Growth _____   Health _____

Friends _____   Family _____   Romance_____

LIFE SATISFACTION ASSESSMENT

On a scale of one (needs work) to ten (fabulous), how would you relate your level of satisfaction in each area of the wheel below?

If an area isn't a "ten," what would make it a ten?

Write your responses on the next page.

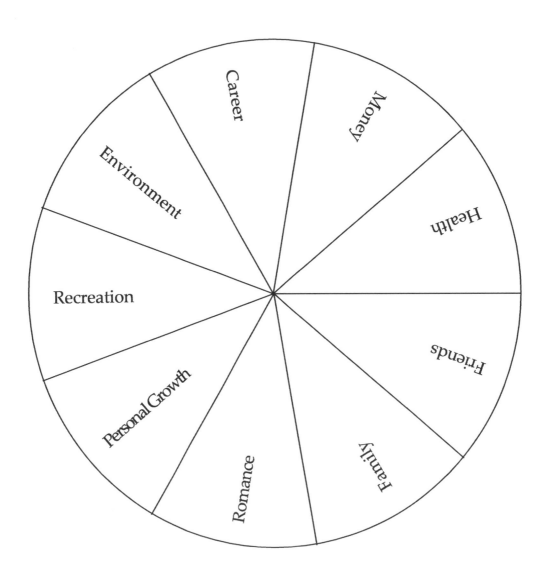

What's the gap between where you are and where you want to be?
What's the next step to move towards your ten?

Career

Money

Health

Friends

Family

Romance

Personal Growth

Recreation

Physical Environment

MAGIC ACCELERATOR

The Magic of Strong Boundaries

"If I won't be myself, who will?"
– Alfred Hitchcock

Strengthening our boundaries is one of the most powerful ways to transform our relationships and improve our lives personally and professionally. This quarter we look at boundaries.

Boundaries let us know the difference between our authentic self and our social self that is based on pleasing others. People with strong boundaries lead happier, more fulfilling lives. We feel confident to speak our truth. We accept what we want, and we reject what we don't want in our lives.

Having strong boundaries is very attractive. Weak boundaries disempower us and disrespect those around us.

Weak boundaries show up in a number of ways:

- The inability to say no.
- The fear of displeasing someone.
- The tendency to rescue others.
- The expectation of being rescued.
- Not expressing our true feelings.
- Attracting people who take advantage of us.
- Allowing outside opinions to determine our self-worth.
- Feeling like a victim.
- Feeling obligated, indebted.
- Trying to change someone else.

So, where do weak boundaries come from?

When we were children, pleasing parents, teachers, and friends was necessary to our survival. We needed to learn how to bond, how to read reactions, how to compromise. These are not skills to give up. This is where we learn the empathy and compassion that makes relationships possible.

Problems arise when, as adults, we are unconsciously ruled by these needs to please, bond, or compromise. We are operating out of fear more than love. When we are acting from unconscious impulses, we give up our ability to choose responsibly, and we become victims and victimizers.

We all have areas in our lives where our boundaries are nice and strong, and other areas where our boundaries get weaker. (The higher the stakes, the stronger the likelihood is that fear will come in and weaken our boundaries.) The easiest way to check the strength of your boundaries is to ask yourself: "How free do I feel here to say what I feel and to ask for what I want?"

This Quarter's invitation:

Take a look at your own life.

Where are your boundaries strongest? Where are they weakest? Why?

What small step can you take to be more honest and authentic in that area of your life?

As you strengthen your boundaries in any area of your life, you will increase your self-confidence. You will attract better relationships. You will enjoy more respect and success.

"To free us from the expectations of others, to give us back to ourselves - therelies the great, singular power of self-respect." ~ **Joan Didion**

Weekly Journal

From _____ to _____.

Top Priorities

These actions are my top priorities this week.
Anything else is for fairy points.

☐ _____

☐ _____

☐ _____

☐ _____

☐ _____

Magic Strategy:

Stronger Boundaries
How will I be respectful of myself?

Challenges

Opportunities

Make Money Happy

_____

Request Assistance from The Universe
What I would like help with this week.

_____

Life Balance: What small step would improve each of these areas of your life?

Career_____ Money_____ Recreation_____

Environment_____ Personal Growth_____ Health_____

Friends_____ Family_____ Romance_____

Success Journal

Monday
1
2
3
4
5
Tuesday
1
2
3
4
5
Wednesday
1
2
3
4
5
Thursday
1
2
3
4
5
Friday
1
2
3
4
5
Saturday
1
2
3
4
5
Sunday
1
2
3
4
5

Make Money Happy Daily

Monday

Tuesday

Wednesday

Thursday

Friday

Saturday

Sunday

Gratitude

What I am grateful for this week:

Learning

What I learned about myself this week:

Weekly Journal

From _____ to _____.

Top Priorities

These actions are my top priorities this week. Anything else is for fairy points.

☐ _____

☐ _____

☐ _____

☐ _____

☐ _____

Make Money Happy

_____

Magic Strategy:

Stronger Boundaries

How will I be respectful of myself?

Challenges

Opportunities

Request Assistance from The Universe

What I would like help with this week.

_____

Life Balance: What small step would improve each of these areas of your life?

Career_____ Money_____ Recreation_____

Environment_____ Personal Growth_____ Health_____

Friends_____ Family_____ Romance_____

Success Journal

Monday
1
2
3
4
5
Tuesday
1
2
3
4
5
Wednesday
1
2
3
4
5
Thursday
1
2
3
4
5
Friday
1
2
3
4
5
Saturday
1
2
3
4
5
Sunday
1
2
3
4
5

Make Money Happy Daily

Monday

Tuesday

Wednesday

Thursday

Friday

Saturday

Sunday

Gratitude

What I am grateful for this week:

Learning

What I learned about myself this week:

Weekly Journal

From _____ to _____.

Top Priorities

These actions are my top priorities this week.
Anything else is for fairy points.

☐ _____

☐ _____

☐ _____

☐ _____

☐ _____

Make Money Happy

_____

Magic Strategy:

Stronger Boundaries

How will I be respectful of myself?

Challenges

Opportunities

Request Assistance from The Universe

What I would like help with this week.

_____

Life Balance: What small step would improve each of these areas of your life?

Career_____ Money_____ Recreation_____

Environment_____ Personal Growth_____ Health_____

Friends_____ Family_____ Romance_____

Success Journal

Monday
1
2
3
4
5
Tuesday
1
2
3
4
5
Wednesday
1
2
3
4
5
Thursday
1
2
3
4
5
Friday
1
2
3
4
5
Saturday
1
2
3
4
5
Sunday
1
2
3
4
5

Make Money Happy Daily

Monday

Tuesday

Wednesday

Thursday

Friday

Saturday

Sunday

Gratitude

What I am grateful for this week:

Learning

What I learned about myself this week:

Weekly Journal

From _____ to _____.

Top Priorities

These actions are my top priorities this week.
Anything else is for fairy points.

☐ _____

☐ _____

☐ _____

☐ _____

☐ _____

Make Money Happy

_____

Magic Strategy:

Stronger Boundaries
How will I be respectful of myself?

Challenges

Opportunities

Request Assistance from The Universe
What I would like help with this week.

_____

Life Balance: What small step would improve each of these areas of your life?

Career_____ Money_____ Recreation_____

Environment_____ Personal Growth_____ Health_____

Friends_____ Family_____ Romance_____

Success Journal

Monday
1
2
3
4
5
Tuesday
1
2
3
4
5
Wednesday
1
2
3
4
5
Thursday
1
2
3
4
5
Friday
1
2
3
4
5
Saturday
1
2
3
4
5
Sunday
1
2
3
4
5

Make Money Happy Daily

Monday

Tuesday

Wednesday

Thursday

Friday

Saturday

Sunday

Gratitude

What I am grateful for this week:

Learning

What I learned about myself this week:

Weekly Journal

From _____ to _____.

Top Priorities

These actions are my top priorities this week.
Anything else is for fairy points.

☐ _____

☐ _____

☐ _____

☐ _____

☐ _____

Make Money Happy

_____

Magic Strategy:

Stronger Boundaries

How will I be respectful of myself?

Challenges

Opportunities

Request Assistance from The Universe

What I would like help with this week.

_____

Life Balance: What small step would improve each of these areas of your life?

Career_____ Money_____ Recreation_____

Environment_____ Personal Growth_____ Health_____

Friends_____ Family_____ Romance_____

Success Journal

Monday
1
2
3
4
5
Tuesday
1
2
3
4
5
Wednesday
1
2
3
4
5
Thursday
1
2
3
4
5
Friday
1
2
3
4
5
Saturday
1
2
3
4
5
Sunday
1
2
3
4
5

Make Money Happy Daily

Monday

Tuesday

Wednesday

Thursday

Friday

Saturday

Sunday

Gratitude

What I am grateful for this week:

Learning

What I learned about myself this week:

Weekly Journal

From _____ to _____.

Top Priorities

These actions are my top priorities this week.
Anything else is for fairy points.

☐ _____

☐ _____

☐ _____

☐ _____

☐ _____

Make Money Happy

_____

Magic Strategy:

Stronger Boundaries

How will I be respectful of myself?

Challenges

Opportunities

Request Assistance from The Universe

What I would like help with this week.

_____

Life Balance: What small step would improve each of these areas of your life?

Career_____ Money_____ Recreation_____

Environment_____ Personal Growth_____ Health_____

Friends_____ Family_____ Romance_____

Success Journal

Monday
1
2
3
4
5
Tuesday
1
2
3
4
5
Wednesday
1
2
3
4
5
Thursday
1
2
3
4
5
Friday
1
2
3
4
5
Saturday
1
2
3
4
5
Sunday
1
2
3
4
5

Make Money Happy Daily

Monday

Tuesday

Wednesday

Thursday

Friday

Saturday

Sunday

Gratitude

What I am grateful for this week:

Learning

What I learned about myself this week:

Weekly Journal

From _____ to _____.

Top Priorities

These actions are my top priorities this week.
Anything else is for fairy points.

☐ _____

☐ _____

☐ _____

☐ _____

☐ _____

Magic Strategy:

Stronger Boundaries

How will I be respectful of myself?

Challenges

Opportunities

Make Money Happy

_____

Request Assistance from The Universe

What I would like help with this week.

_____

Life Balance: What small step would improve each of these areas of your life?

Career_____   Money_____   Recreation_____

Environment_____   Personal Growth_____   Health_____

Friends_____   Family_____   Romance_____

Success Journal

Monday
1
2
3
4
5
Tuesday
1
2
3
4
5
Wednesday
1
2
3
4
5
Thursday
1
2
3
4
5
Friday
1
2
3
4
5
Saturday
1
2
3
4
5
Sunday
1
2
3
4
5

Make Money Happy Daily

Monday

Tuesday

Wednesday

Thursday

Friday

Saturday

Sunday

Gratitude

What I am grateful for this week:

Learning

What I learned about myself this week:

 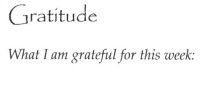

Weekly Journal

From _____ to _____.

Top Priorities

These actions are my top priorities this week. Anything else is for fairy points.

☐ _____

☐ _____

☐ _____

☐ _____

☐ _____

Make Money Happy

_____

Magic Strategy:

Stronger Boundaries

How will I be respectful of myself?

Challenges

Opportunities

Request Assistance from The Universe

What I would like help with this week.

_____

Life Balance: What small step would improve each of these areas of your life?

Career_____ Money_____ Recreation_____

Environment_____ Personal Growth_____ Health_____

Friends_____ Family_____ Romance_____

Success Journal

Monday
1
2
3
4
5
Tuesday
1
2
3
4
5
Wednesday
1
2
3
4
5
Thursday
1
2
3
4
5
Friday
1
2
3
4
5
Saturday
1
2
3
4
5
Sunday
1
2
3
4
5

Make Money Happy Daily

Monday

Tuesday

Wednesday

Thursday

Friday

Saturday

Sunday

Gratitude

What I am grateful for this week:

Learning

What I learned about myself this week:

Weekly Journal

From _____ to _____.

Top Priorities

These actions are my top priorities this week.
Anything else is for fairy points.

☐ _____

☐ _____

☐ _____

☐ _____

☐ _____

Make Money Happy

_____

Magic Strategy:

Stronger Boundaries

How will I be respectful of myself?

Challenges

Opportunities

Request Assistance from The Universe

What I would like help with this week.

_____

Life Balance: What small step would improve each of these areas of your life?

Career_____ Money_____ Recreation_____

Environment_____ Personal Growth_____ Health_____

Friends_____ Family_____ Romance_____

Success Journal

Monday
1
2
3
4
5
Tuesday
1
2
3
4
5
Wednesday
1
2
3
4
5
Thursday
1
2
3
4
5
Friday
1
2
3
4
5
Saturday
1
2
3
4
5
Sunday
1
2
3
4
5

Make Money Happy Daily

Monday

Tuesday

Wednesday

Thursday

Friday

Saturday

Sunday

Gratitude

What I am grateful for this week:

Learning

What I learned about myself this week:

Weekly Journal

From _____ to _____.

Top Priorities

These actions are my top priorities this week.
Anything else is for fairy points.

☐ _____

☐ _____

☐ _____

☐ _____

☐ _____

Magic Strategy:

Stronger Boundaries

How will I be respectful of myself?

Challenges

Opportunities

Make Money Happy

_____

Request Assistance from The Universe

What I would like help with this week.

Life Balance: What small step would improve each of these areas of your life?

Career_____ Money_____ Recreation_____

Environment_____ Personal Growth_____ Health_____

Friends_____ Family_____ Romance_____

Success Journal

Monday
1
2
3
4
5
Tuesday
1
2
3
4
5
Wednesday
1
2
3
4
5
Thursday
1
2
3
4
5
Friday
1
2
3
4
5
Saturday
1
2
3
4
5
Sunday
1
2
3
4
5

Make Money Happy Daily

Monday

Tuesday

Wednesday

Thursday

Friday

Saturday

Sunday

Gratitude

What I am grateful for this week:

Learning

What I learned about myself this week:

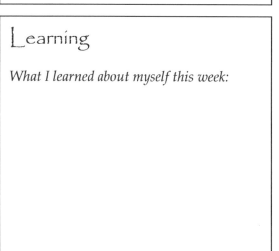

Weekly Journal

From _____ to _____.

Top Priorities

These actions are my top priorities this week.
Anything else is for fairy points.

☐ _____

☐ _____

☐ _____

☐ _____

☐ _____

Make Money Happy

_____

Magic Strategy:

Stronger Boundaries

How will I be respectful of myself?

Challenges

Opportunities

Request Assistance from The Universe

What I would like help with this week.

_____

Life Balance: What small step would improve each of these areas of your life?

Career_____   Money_____   Recreation_____

Environment_____   Personal Growth_____   Health_____

Friends_____   Family_____   Romance_____

Success Journal

Monday
1
2
3
4
5
Tuesday
1
2
3
4
5
Wednesday
1
2
3
4
5
Thursday
1
2
3
4
5
Friday
1
2
3
4
5
Saturday
1
2
3
4
5
Sunday
1
2
3
4
5

Make Money Happy Daily

Monday

Tuesday

Wednesday

Thursday

Friday

Saturday

Sunday

Gratitude

What I am grateful for this week:

Learning

What I learned about myself this week:

Weekly Journal

From _____ to _____.

Top Priorities

These actions are my top priorities this week.
Anything else is for fairy points.

☐ _____

☐ _____

☐ _____

☐ _____

☐ _____

Make Money Happy

_____

Magic Strategy:

Stronger Boundaries

How will I be respectful of myself?

Challenges

Opportunities

Request Assistance from The Universe

What I would like help with this week.

_____

Life Balance: What small step would improve each of these areas of your life?

Career_____ Money_____ Recreation_____

Environment_____ Personal Growth_____ Health_____

Friends_____ Family_____ Romance_____

Success Journal

Monday
1
2
3
4
5
Tuesday
1
2
3
4
5
Wednesday
1
2
3
4
5
Thursday
1
2
3
4
5
Friday
1
2
3
4
5
Saturday
1
2
3
4
5
Sunday
1
2
3
4
5

Make Money Happy Daily

Monday

Tuesday

Wednesday

Thursday

Friday

Saturday

Sunday

Gratitude

What I am grateful for this week:

Learning

What I learned about myself this week:

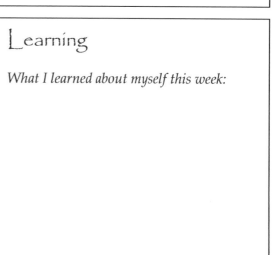

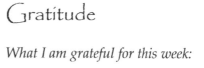

Weekly Journal

From _____ to _____.

Top Priorities

These actions are my top priorities this week.
Anything else is for fairy points.

☐ _____

☐ _____

☐ _____

☐ _____

☐ _____

Make Money Happy

_____

Magic Strategy:

Stronger Boundaries

How will I be respectful of myself?

Challenges

Opportunities

Request Assistance from The Universe

What I would like help with this week.

_____

Life Balance: What small step would improve each of these areas of your life?

Career_____   Money_____   Recreation_____

Environment_____   Personal Growth_____   Health_____

Friends_____   Family_____   Romance_____

Success Journal

Monday
1
2
3
4
5
Tuesday
1
2
3
4
5
Wednesday
1
2
3
4
5
Thursday
1
2
3
4
5
Friday
1
2
3
4
5
Saturday
1
2
3
4
5
Sunday
1
2
3
4
5

Make Money Happy Daily

Monday

Tuesday

Wednesday

Thursday

Friday

Saturday

Sunday

Gratitude

What I am grateful for this week:

Learning

What I learned about myself this week:

THIRD QUARTER HIGHLIGHTS
AND LEARNINGS

Accomplishments	What I Learned	Next Step

What did I do really well this quarter?

In what area of my life did I grow the most?

What is the most important thing I learned about myself?

How can I give myself even better results in the future?

Fourth Quarter

❖ ❖ ❖

"I want to begin by thanking you for the amazing work you are doing. I very much look forward to working with you in the future and sharing even more amazing stories like the one I want to share now.

I first heard you on the World Puja interview you did a few months back. I was so captivated by your ideas that I listened to the interview twice through, ordered the book that night, and told several friends about you in an e-mail. That night, I went to sleep thinking about money, who money is to me, and feeling really GOOD about money.

The next day, I got home from work, and in the mail was money! Not bills, but money! There were two small rebate checks AND a child support check from my 19 year old daughter's father. What is truly amazing is that I had not received child support from him since she was 3 years old! It has been coming faithfully ever since. I remembered to thank money!

Today we had an appointment to speak for the first time, and just before speaking with you, I received an e-mail from a woman who wants to GIVE me $500 to support my work as a children's yoga teacher! This is really quite a love affair that's unfolding.

With great appreciation and gratitude to you, Ms. Match-Maker, I tip my hat!"
— Margot Dengel

❖ ❖ ❖

NOTES

Fourth Quarter Intentions

Eliminate Tolerations

Stop settling! What energy and joy drainers are you ready to handle?

Workplace

Home & Personal

Make A Wish

What's the big thing you want to have happen this quarter?

This Year's Theme

_____

Magic Accelerator

Stronger Boundaries
Success by Association

1.

2.

3.

Top Three Personal Goals

1.

2.

3.

Life Balance: What small step would improve each area of your Life Wheel?

Career _____   Money _____   Recreation _____

Environment _____   Personal Growth _____   Health _____

Friends _____   Family _____   Romance_____

LIFE SATISFACTION ASSESSMENT

On a scale of one (needs work) to ten (fabulous), how would you relate your level of satisfaction in each area of the wheel below?

If an area isn't a "ten," what would make it a ten?

Write your responses on the next page.

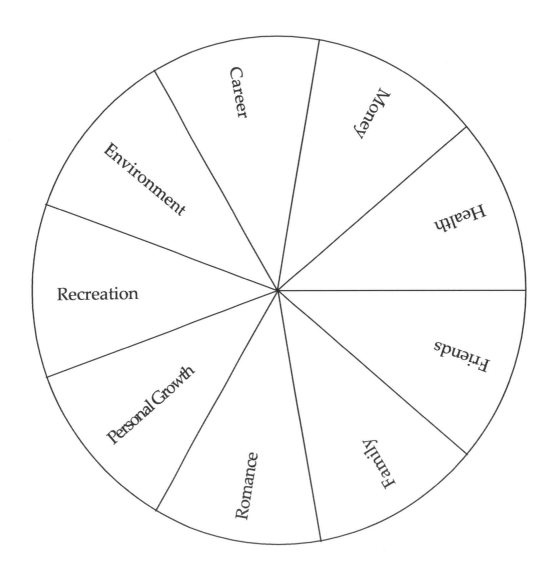

What's the gap between where you are and where you want to be? What's the next step to move towards your ten?

Career

Money

Health

Friends

Family

Romance

Personal Growth

Recreation

Physical Environment

MAGIC ACCELERATOR

Success by Association

"The greatest genius will never be worth much if he pretends to draw exclusively from his own resources."

~ Johann Wolfgang von Goethe

I have a confession.

I was a nerd in grade school. I was that nerdy girl wearing the polyester "floods" from Pic'n Save. I kept my nose in books like *Jane Eyre* or *Lord of the Rings*. Small talk baffled me.

Then in the sixth grade, two popular girls adopted me. They took me to the mall and taught me how to dress, became my friends, and included me in their activities. Soon I was learning how to make friends, flirt and hold my own with the "cool" kids, (politically active, articulate, popular, musically hip), I admired.

What happened? These two girls pulled me up to their level of social finesse by association. And these girls were great people–smart, socially aware, responsible, and compassionate human beings. People I admire to this day. Our values meshed, and they knew something I needed to learn about social rapport.

> "WOW...Sistah...since committing to your online Financial Alchemy Academy Program...
>
> 2 speeding tickets I got came back as cheques in my name in the mail as the Court of Queens' Bench deemed them inappropriate (when does that ever happen????),
>
> unexpected $2300 Income Tax return credit to me, increased my pricing and packaging this morning and
>
> sold my first new and improved ultimate package for $1575 this afternoon,
>
> not ONE but TWO offers on our house.....
>
> not to mention so many other gracious acts of kindness all around me....This stuff is magic and so am I....sending love...."
>
> - Linda Crawford
> Alberta, Canada

And this brings us to this Quarter's Accelerator:

Success by Association. One of the easiest, quickest, and most effective ways to ensure change is to surround yourself with people who will pull you into your future. Look for people who reflect who you want to become. They have accomplished their goal or are well on their way.

Here are some ideas:

Want to lose weight and get healthy? Make friends with people who eat healthy and work out.

Want to increase your sales? Hang out with people who are great at sales. Want more inner peace? Spend time with peaceful friends.

Want to be a millionaire? Get yourself into a group of millionaires.

Would you like to be a kinder, happier person? Find yourself some kind, happy people. Consider joining a charity.

And this is key: **Celebrate the successes of your friends!** Their success shows you that you are getting closer. The more successful your friends are, the more successful you will be too!

Why this works:

What is around you becomes more real, more normal. You start to think like your comrades.

You don't have to fight the pull of a negative environment. A community of people who are what you want to become creates an energetic momentum that carries you forward.

This new reality becomes imprinted in your unconscious. You are moving forward even when you are not consciously "working" at it.

My invitation to you:

Notice where you spend your time.

How can you surround yourself with people who will help you move forward?

Weekly Journal

From _____ to _____.

Top Priorities

These actions are my top priorities this week.
Anything else is for fairy points.

☐ _____

☐ _____

☐ _____

☐ _____

☐ _____

Make Money Happy

_____

Magic Strategy:

Success by Association

Spend time with Success.

Challenges

Opportunities

Request Assistance from The Universe

What I would like help with this week.

_____

Life Balance: What small step would improve each of these areas of your life?

Career_____ Money_____ Recreation_____

Environment_____ Personal Growth_____ Health_____

Friends_____ Family_____ Romance_____

Success Journal

Monday
1
2
3
4
5
Tuesday
1
2
3
4
5
Wednesday
1
2
3
4
5
Thursday
1
2
3
4
5
Friday
1
2
3
4
5
Saturday
1
2
3
4
5
Sunday
1
2
3
4
5

Make Money Happy Daily

Monday

Tuesday

Wednesday

Thursday

Friday

Saturday

Sunday

Gratitude

What I am grateful for this week:

Learning

What I learned about myself this week:

Weekly Journal

From _____ to _____.

Top Priorities

These actions are my top priorities this week.
Anything else is for fairy points.

☐ _____

☐ _____

☐ _____

☐ _____

☐ _____

Magic Strategy:

Success by Association

Spend time with Success.

Challenges

Opportunities

Make Money Happy

_____

Request Assistance from The Universe

What I would like help with this week.

_____

Life Balance: What small step would improve each of these areas of your life?

Career_____ Money_____ Recreation_____

Environment_____ Personal Growth_____ Health_____

Friends_____ Family_____ Romance_____

Success Journal

Monday
1
2
3
4
5
Tuesday
1
2
3
4
5
Wednesday
1
2
3
4
5
Thursday
1
2
3
4
5
Friday
1
2
3
4
5
Saturday
1
2
3
4
5
Sunday
1
2
3
4
5

Make Money Happy Daily

Monday

Tuesday

Wednesday

Thursday

Friday

Saturday

Sunday

Gratitude

What I am grateful for this week:

Learning

What I learned about myself this week:

Weekly Journal

From _____ to _____.

Top Priorities

These actions are my top priorities this week.
Anything else is for fairy points.

☐ _____

☐ _____

☐ _____

☐ _____

☐ _____

Make Money Happy

_____

Magic Strategy:

Success by Association

Spend time with Success.

Challenges

Opportunities

Request Assistance from The Universe

What I would like help with this week.

_____

Life Balance: What small step would improve each of these areas of your life?

Career_____ Money_____ Recreation_____

Environment_____ Personal Growth_____ Health_____

Friends_____ Family_____ Romance_____

Success Journal

Monday
1
2
3
4
5
Tuesday
1
2
3
4
5
Wednesday
1
2
3
4
5
Thursday
1
2
3
4
5
Friday
1
2
3
4
5
Saturday
1
2
3
4
5
Sunday
1
2
3
4
5

Make Money Happy Daily

Monday

Tuesday

Wednesday

Thursday

Friday

Saturday

Sunday

Gratitude

What I am grateful for this week:

Learning

What I learned about myself this week:

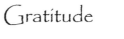

Weekly Journal

From _____ to _____.

Top Priorities

These actions are my top priorities this week.
Anything else is for fairy points.

☐ _____

☐ _____

☐ _____

☐ _____

☐ _____

Magic Strategy:

Success by Association

Spend time with Success.

Challenges

Opportunities

Make Money Happy

_____

Request Assistance

from The Universe

What I would like help with this week.

_____

Life Balance: What small step would improve each of these areas of your life?

Career_____ Money_____ Recreation_____

Environment_____ Personal Growth_____ Health_____

Friends_____ Family_____ Romance_____

Success Journal

Monday
1
2
3
4
5
Tuesday
1
2
3
4
5
Wednesday
1
2
3
4
5
Thursday
1
2
3
4
5
Friday
1
2
3
4
5
Saturday
1
2
3
4
5
Sunday
1
2
3
4
5

Make Money Happy Daily

Monday

Tuesday

Wednesday

Thursday

Friday

Saturday

Sunday

Gratitude

What I am grateful for this week:

Learning

What I learned about myself this week:

Weekly Journal

From _____ to _____.

Top Priorities

These actions are my top priorities this week.
Anything else is for fairy points.

☐ _____

☐ _____

☐ _____

☐ _____

☐ _____

Magic Strategy:

Success by Association
Spend time with Success.

Challenges

Opportunities

Make Money Happy

_____

Request Assistance from The Universe

What I would like help with this week.

_____

Life Balance: What small step would improve each of these areas of your life?

Career_____ Money_____ Recreation_____

Environment_____ Personal Growth_____ Health_____

Friends_____ Family_____ Romance_____

Success Journal

Monday
1
2
3
4
5
Tuesday
1
2
3
4
5
Wednesday
1
2
3
4
5
Thursday
1
2
3
4
5
Friday
1
2
3
4
5
Saturday
1
2
3
4
5
Sunday
1
2
3
4
5

Make Money Happy Daily

Monday

Tuesday

Wednesday

Thursday

Friday

Saturday

Sunday

Gratitude

What I am grateful for this week:

Learning

What I learned about myself this week:

Weekly Journal

From _____ to _____.

Top Priorities

These actions are my top priorities this week.
Anything else is for fairy points.

☐ _____

☐ _____

☐ _____

☐ _____

☐ _____

Magic Strategy:

Success by Association

Spend time with Success.

Challenges

Opportunities

Make Money Happy

_____

Request Assistance from The Universe

What I would like help with this week.

_____

Life Balance: What small step would improve each of these areas of your life?

Career_____ Money_____ Recreation_____

Environment_____ Personal Growth_____ Health_____

Friends_____ Family_____ Romance_____

Success Journal

Monday
1
2
3
4
5
Tuesday
1
2
3
4
5
Wednesday
1
2
3
4
5
Thursday
1
2
3
4
5
Friday
1
2
3
4
5
Saturday
1
2
3
4
5
Sunday
1
2
3
4
5

Make Money Happy Daily

Monday

Tuesday

Wednesday

Thursday

Friday

Saturday

Sunday

Gratitude

What I am grateful for this week:

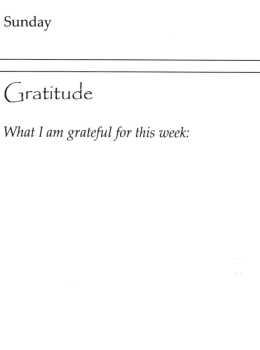

Learning

What I learned about myself this week:

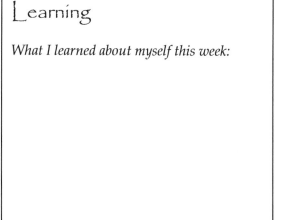

Weekly Journal

From _____ to _____.

Top Priorities

These actions are my top priorities this week.
Anything else is for fairy points.

☐ _____

☐ _____

☐ _____

☐ _____

☐ _____

Magic Strategy:

Success by Association

Spend time with Success.

Challenges

Opportunities

Make Money Happy

_____

Request Assistance from The Universe

What I would like help with this week.

_____

Life Balance: What small step would improve each of these areas of your life?

Career_____ Money_____ Recreation_____

Environment_____ Personal Growth_____ Health_____

Friends_____ Family_____ Romance_____

Success Journal

Monday
1
2
3
4
5
Tuesday
1
2
3
4
5
Wednesday
1
2
3
4
5
Thursday
1
2
3
4
5
Friday
1
2
3
4
5
Saturday
1
2
3
4
5
Sunday
1
2
3
4
5

Make Money Happy Daily

Monday

Tuesday

Wednesday

Thursday

Friday

Saturday

Sunday

Gratitude

What I am grateful for this week:

Learning

What I learned about myself this week:

Weekly Journal

From _____ to _____.

Top Priorities

These actions are my top priorities this week.
Anything else is for fairy points.

☐ _____

☐ _____

☐ _____

☐ _____

☐ _____

Make Money Happy

_____

Magic Strategy:

Success by Association

Spend time with Success.

Challenges

Opportunities

Request Assistance from The Universe

What I would like help with this week.

_____

Life Balance: What small step would improve each of these areas of your life?

Career_____ Money_____ Recreation_____

Environment_____ Personal Growth_____ Health_____

Friends_____ Family_____ Romance_____

Success Journal

Monday
1
2
3
4
5
Tuesday
1
2
3
4
5
Wednesday
1
2
3
4
5
Thursday
1
2
3
4
5
Friday
1
2
3
4
5
Saturday
1
2
3
4
5
Sunday
1
2
3
4
5

Make Money Happy Daily

Monday

Tuesday

Wednesday

Thursday

Friday

Saturday

Sunday

Gratitude

What I am grateful for this week:

Learning

What I learned about myself this week:

Weekly Journal

From _____ to _____.

Top Priorities

These actions are my top priorities this week. Anything else is for fairy points.

☐ _____

☐ _____

☐ _____

☐ _____

☐ _____

Make Money Happy

_____

Magic Strategy:

Success by Association

Spend time with Success.

Challenges

Opportunities

Request Assistance from The Universe

What I would like help with this week.

_____

Life Balance: What small step would improve each of these areas of your life?

Career_____ Money_____ Recreation_____

Environment_____ Personal Growth_____ Health_____

Friends_____ Family_____ Romance_____

Success Journal

Monday
1
2
3
4
5
Tuesday
1
2
3
4
5
Wednesday
1
2
3
4
5
Thursday
1
2
3
4
5
Friday
1
2
3
4
5
Saturday
1
2
3
4
5
Sunday
1
2
3
4
5

Make Money Happy Daily

Monday

Tuesday

Wednesday

Thursday

Friday

Saturday

Sunday

Gratitude

What I am grateful for this week:

Learning

What I learned about myself this week:

Weekly Journal

From _____ to _____.

Top Priorities

These actions are my top priorities this week.
Anything else is for fairy points.

☐ _____

☐ _____

☐ _____

☐ _____

☐ _____

Make Money Happy

_____

Magic Strategy:

Success by Association

Spend time with Success.

Challenges

Opportunities

Request Assistance from The Universe

What I would like help with this week.

_____

Life Balance: What small step would improve each of these areas of your life?

Career_____   Money_____   Recreation_____

Environment_____   Personal Growth_____   Health_____

Friends_____   Family_____   Romance_____

Success Journal

Monday
1
2
3
4
5
Tuesday
1
2
3
4
5
Wednesday
1
2
3
4
5
Thursday
1
2
3
4
5
Friday
1
2
3
4
5
Saturday
1
2
3
4
5
Sunday
1
2
3
4
5

Make Money Happy Daily

Monday

Tuesday

Wednesday

Thursday

Friday

Saturday

Sunday

Gratitude

What I am grateful for this week:

Learning

What I learned about myself this week:

Weekly Journal

From _____ to _____.

Top Priorities

These actions are my top priorities this week.
Anything else is for fairy points.

☐ _____

☐ _____

☐ _____

☐ _____

☐ _____

Magic Strategy:

Success by Association

Spend time with Success.

Challenges

Opportunities

Make Money Happy

_____

Request Assistance from The Universe

What I would like help with this week.

_____

Life Balance: What small step would improve each of these areas of your life?

Career_____   Money_____   Recreation_____

Environment_____   Personal Growth_____   Health_____

Friends_____   Family_____   Romance_____

Success Journal

Monday
1
2
3
4
5
Tuesday
1
2
3
4
5
Wednesday
1
2
3
4
5
Thursday
1
2
3
4
5
Friday
1
2
3
4
5
Saturday
1
2
3
4
5
Sunday
1
2
3
4
5

Make Money Happy Daily

Monday

Tuesday

Wednesday

Thursday

Friday

Saturday

Sunday

Gratitude

What I am grateful for this week:

Learning

What I learned about myself this week:

Weekly Journal

From _____ to _____.

Top Priorities

These actions are my top priorities this week. Anything else is for fairy points.

☐ _____

☐ _____

☐ _____

☐ _____

☐ _____

Make Money Happy

_____

Magic Strategy:

Success by Association

Spend time with Success.

Challenges

Opportunities

Request Assistance from The Universe

What I would like help with this week.

_____

Life Balance: What small step would improve each of these areas of your life?

Career_____ Money_____ Recreation_____

Environment_____ Personal Growth_____ Health_____

Friends_____ Family_____ Romance_____

Success Journal

Monday
1
2
3
4
5
Tuesday
1
2
3
4
5
Wednesday
1
2
3
4
5
Thursday
1
2
3
4
5
Friday
1
2
3
4
5
Saturday
1
2
3
4
5
Sunday
1
2
3
4
5

Make Money Happy Daily

Monday

Tuesday

Wednesday

Thursday

Friday

Saturday

Sunday

Gratitude

What I am grateful for this week:

Learning

What I learned about myself this week:

Weekly Journal

From _____ to _____.

Top Priorities

These actions are my top priorities this week.
Anything else is for fairy points.

☐ _____

☐ _____

☐ _____

☐ _____

☐ _____

Make Money Happy

_____

Magic Strategy:

Success by Association

Spend time with Success.

Challenges

Opportunities

Request Assistance from The Universe

What I would like help with this week.

_____

Life Balance: What small step would improve each of these areas of your life?

Career_____ Money_____ Recreation_____

Environment_____ Personal Growth_____ Health_____

Friends_____ Family_____ Romance_____

Success Journal

Monday
1
2
3
4
5
Tuesday
1
2
3
4
5
Wednesday
1
2
3
4
5
Thursday
1
2
3
4
5
Friday
1
2
3
4
5
Saturday
1
2
3
4
5
Sunday
1
2
3
4
5

Make Money Happy Daily

Monday

Tuesday

Wednesday

Thursday

Friday

Saturday

Sunday

Gratitude

What I am grateful for this week:

Learning

What I learned about myself this week:

FOURTH QUARTER HIGHLIGHTS
AND LEARNINGS

Accomplishments	What I Learned	Next Step

What did I do really well this quarter?

In what area of my life did I grow the most?

What is the most important thing I learned about myself?

COMPLETION

Congratulations! It's time to celebrate your success.

1) How did your life change this year?

2) What are you most proud of?

3) What are you most grateful for?

4) What did you learn about money?

5) What did you learn about manifesting?

6) What's next?

If there is anything left over from this year that you don't want to take into the next, write it down, declare it complete, and flush it away!

Go out and CELEBRATE, REWARD YOURSELF, MAKE MAGIC!

NOTES

ABOUT THE AUTHOR

Morgana Rae is an internationally acclaimed life coach, author, and professional speaker, and she is regarded to be the world's top Relationship with Money coach. Morgana's groundbreaking program for attracting wealth has featured her in *Entrepreneur* Magazine, *United Press International, The Wall Street Journal,* and Coast to Coast Radio. She was a recurring "Money Maven" on FOX-TV.

A certified Master Results Coach and mythologist trained in NLP, hypnosis, and co-active coaching, Morgana draws on these skills and over 20 years in the entertainment industry to create fun, dynamic exercises that transform your life quickly—with stunning results. She's the owner of Charmed Life Coaching®, a successful life and business coaching company. Morgana has coached thousands of clients, many as far away as Scotland, Singapore, India and Australia. She's a recognized leader in the coaching profession.

Morgana also speaks professionally in locales from Baja, California to Oslo, Norway. She's been a featured expert with Marci Shimoff, Arielle Ford, Deepak Chopra, John Gray, John Assaraf, Arianna Huffington, and many others.

Morgana's fans have called her a "Money Goddess" because of the many documented stories of clients manifesting unexpected income of hundreds, thousands, hundreds of thousands and even more, often within hours of implementing her signature Financial Alchemy® process.

Morgana's Financial Alchemy® books, CDs, magazine articles, and classes have impacted the lives of hundreds of thousands of people worldwide. Morgana writes, speaks, and coaches from a desire to empower idealistic entrepreneurs, coaches, authors and artists to have a big impact in the world... and to heal the rift between heart, spirit, and money.

Share Your Story!

Do YOU have a Financial Alchemy success story? Share your story and **win a chance to be featured on www.AlchemySuccess.com.**

Will you be my next success story?

Send a written email or a video link to wecare@morganarae.com.

Please include a photo and a web link if you wish to get further visibility for yourself or your business!

Made in the USA
Las Vegas, NV
23 January 2023

66146985R00109